MW00719209

# Miss Brocklehurst on the Nile

# MISS BROCKLEHURST ON THE NILE

*Diary of a Victorian traveller in Egypt*

Millrace

First published in Great Britain in 2004 by
Millrace
2a Leafield Road, Disley
Cheshire SK12 2JF


Marianne Brocklehurst's text and illustrations
© 2004 Macclesfield Borough Council
Illustrated map © 2004 Jane Droop
Introduction © 2004 Millrace

ISBN: 1 902173 147




Typeset in Book Antiqua.
Produced in the United Kingdom by
LPPS Ltd, Wellingborough, Northants NN8 3PJ

# Contents

# Acknowledgements

We would like to thank Macclesfield Borough Council and Macclesfield Museums Trust for their co-operation in allowing publication of this diary. Richard de Peyer and Louanne Collins, Director and former Director of Macclesfield Silk Museums, have been consistently helpful and enthusiastic; Mark Wheelton, Head of the Borough's Leisure Services, and Vicky Fox of the Legal Department ensured that the preliminary difficulties were smoothed out.

We would also like to express our gratitude to Kate Reeder for generously making available her detailed research into Marianne Brocklehurst's life; to Rosalie and Antony David for so promptly and expertly fielding queries relating to Egyptology and Arabic; and to Jane Droop for drawing a delightful map of Marianne's route up the Nile.

# Introduction

At Shepheard's, Cairo, in 1873 a shifting mass of foreigners gathered daily to enjoy the hotel's ancient glories, endure its cooking and discuss arrangements for a trip up the Nile. The river bobbed with the boats of British and American travellers; the wealthy chartered dahabeeyahs, the rest piled onto Cook's steamers. A Nile voyage was *the* winter pastime. For a public already captivated by descriptions of Mariette Bey's archaeological digs, the Prince and Princess of Wales' tour up the river the year before had set the seal of approval. At the hotel, travel writer and novelist Amelia Edwards crisply categorised her fellow tourists as

*invalids in search of health; artists in search of subjects; sportsmen keen upon crocodiles; statesmen out for a holiday; special correspondents alert for gossip; collectors on the scent of papyri and mummies; men of science with only scientific ends in view; and the usual surplus of idlers who travel for the mere love of travel or the satisfaction of a purposeless curiosity.*[1]

One of the tourists, with characteristic aplomb, managed to occupy several of the categories at once. At 41, Miss Marianne Brocklehurst was a competent artist and sportswoman, an avid collector of antiquities and an indefatigable traveller. She was also an Egyptologist. Accompanied by her friend Mary Booth, her nephew Alfred and her groom George, she had arrived in Cairo from Cheshire at the end of November.

The Brocklehursts were wealthy Macclesfield Unitarians, their fortune drawn from silk mills, banking and judicious marriages. Marianne, the youngest of six, was born in 1832, the year her father John was elected one of the town's first MPs. She grew up in a warm, lively family, with a staunch network of cousins, uncles and aunts. Emma, her only sister, was educated in London and presented at court but returned to Macclesfield to teach Marianne. Despite a ten-year age gap, the two were very close. After Emma's marriage and their mother's death, Marianne spent much time in Worcestershire with her sister and brother-in-law, John Dent. She was now of marriageable age and, according to her sister,[2] much sought after. (A portrait painted of her around this time shows a slight, alert figure on horseback.) She enjoyed the social whirl but rejected the suitors, including the Tiverton MP, Heathcote Amory.

Marianne's appetite for travel was sharpened in 1852, when the Dents bore her off to Europe—the first of many such trips. The sisters also took their summer holidays together. In the Lake District, undismayed by a carriage accident, Marianne climbed Skiddaw; in Wales she indulged her passions for fishing and photography. She was also becoming increasingly interested in archaeology. In 1863, when the remains of a Roman villa were found at Sudeley Castle (the estate in Gloucestershire which John Dent had inherited a few years earlier) Marianne was closely involved in the excavations.

But by this time relations between the sisters had cooled. Henry Coventry, nephew of the Hon. Tom Coventry, had proposed to Marianne in 1860 and been accepted. Emma was delighted but John Brocklehurst was not. For him, aristocratic connections in no way compensated for a lack of property. Worse, the head of the family, the young earl, showed a distressing predilection for the turf. John refused his consent and Emma found it hard to forgive the meekness with which Marianne accepted her father's decision.

Further loosening of the ties occurred when Marianne became a professional photographer. Her business partner — and inseparable companion for the rest of her life — was Mary Isabella Booth, who came from an old Yorkshire family. In 1870, Marianne used a legacy from her uncle to build a house, Bagstones, on her brother's estate near Macclesfield. There she and Mary, known jointly as the MBs, lived when they were not roaming the world and it was from there that they set out on their first visit to Egypt.

Marianne's diary begins on 11 November 1873, as they cross the Channel after despatching a monumental amount of luggage. The two women tackle travelling with enormous gusto. Just to read their programme for a single day's sightseeing in Paris is exhausting — but they blithely set off for Turin that same evening.

As they surge on through Italy, the diary becomes increasingly engaging. Marianne's style is dashing and brisk, laced with dry humour. She appreciates landscape and architecture but also has a keen eye for male beauty:

*Strolled through the market and saw some splendid brigands — 15 or 20 — hanging together suspiciously. Found them very attractive and our*

> *admiration became so evident that the old capo di*
> *bande took the opportunity of getting a shilling*
> *out of us.*

Later, chartering a boat in Cairo, she is incensed to find 'a very miserable specimen substituted for our fine Nubian Reis (captain). This we will not stand and have a great row about it at the Consulate with Watson.'

The immediate outcome is not clear but Marianne is happy with their eventual crew and gives a pithy, affectionate description of the men:

> *There is the steersman, Reis Mahommet (2nd Reis*
> *but really first in command), a Nubian of deep*
> *die, a merry excitable fellow, an excellent sailor*
> *and soon a great favourite with us all, Joseph,*
> *who talkee leetle Engliz, Fodle (virtue) a strong*
> *made Nubian, blue black, Hadji Mahommed, 'the*
> *responsible', and little Osman, surnamed Gog-*
> *gles, the smallest man with the biggest spirit on*
> *the boat, afterwards revered by all in his various*
> *capacities of desperate swimmer, sailor, washer-*
> *woman and dress-maker. Abdallah, the good tem-*
> *pered, and four others of no particular attractions,*
> *a serpenty gentleman, Cook, at £12 a month, and*
> *a melancholly [sic] man called the Marmeton or*
> *kitchen maid complete our crew.*

For an account of George, the Brocklehursts' manservant, however, we have to look elsewhere. The MBs first meet writer Amelia Edwards and her companion Miss Renshawe on the crossing from Brindisi. They become friends and arrange to travel in convoy up the Nile. While Marianne is not writing with an eye to publication but to provide a private, family record, Amelia Edwards is a professional. Her comprehensive and scholarly account of the trip, *A Thousand Miles up the Nile*, was published in 1877 and her occasional references to the Brocklehurst party shed light on Marianne's own narrative. Amelia is particularly taken with George:

> [T]he most amazing and incongruous personage in our whole procession is unquestionably George. Now George is an English north-country groom whom the MBs have brought out from the wilds of Lancashire, partly because he is a good shot and may be useful to 'Master Alfred' after birds and crocodiles; and partly from a well-founded belief in his general abilities. And George, who is a fellow of infinite jest and infinite resource, takes to Eastern life as a duckling to the water. He picks up Arabic as if it were his mother tongue. He skins birds like a practised

*taxidermist. He can even wash and iron on occasion. He is, in short, groom, footman, housemaid, laundry-maid, stroke oar, gamekeeper, and general factotum all in one. And beside all this, he is gifted with a comic gravity that no surprises and no disasters can upset for a moment. To see this worthy anachronism cantering along in his groom's coat and gaiters, livery buttons, spotted neckcloth, tall hat, and all the rest of it; his long legs dangling within an inch of the ground on either side of the most diminutive of donkeys; his doubled-barrelled fowling piece under his arm, and that imperturbable look in his face, one would have sworn that he and Egypt were friends of old and that he had been brought up on pyramids from his earliest childhood.*

George's 'infinite jest' even (as reported by an amused Marianne in Nubia) extends to entertaining the crews by 'performing the Arab dance with all its wriggles, to the sound of the tumtum and tamborine, and dressed in proper Arab togs!'

Overshadowed by such resourcefulness and beset by redoubtable middle-aged ladies, it is not surprising that Marianne's nephew, Alfred, emerges a faintly petulant figure. His passion is shooting, his consuming desire to return in triumph in a boat garlanded with dead crocodiles. In the meantime he blazes away at anything he can: ibis, hoopoes, quail, black kingfishers, sand grouse, bee-eaters, plovers, pigeons, a vulture, jackals. On one memorable occasion, his aunt laconically notes, he even shoots 'a native instead of his quail—he quails! But the native recovers and the village is satisfied with three shillings backsheesh, which seems cheap for a man.' Misfortune dogs Alfred. His portmanteau goes astray in Italy, wild geese melt unsportingly away at his approach, he feels unwell. Worse, crocodiles are unaccountably thin on the ground. When at last he shoots one, the carcass fails to resurface, even though they wait hopefully for days.

The boat that Alfred hopes to festoon with dead reptiles is, naturally, a dahabeeyah. As Amelia Edwards notes:

*The choice between dahabeeyah and steamer is like the choice between travelling with post-horses and travelling by rail. The one is expensive, leisurely, delightful; the other is cheap, swift and comparatively comfortless. Those who are content to snatch but a glimpse of the Nile will doubtless prefer the steamer.*

She describes dahabeeyahs as 'not very unlike the

Noah's Ark of our childhood', shallow and flat-bottomed, adapted for sailing or rowing, with cabins on deck and a raised, 'open-air drawing-room'. Amelia charters the Philae, which has white-and-gold panelled walls and ceilings, cushioned divans, bookcases, gilt mirrors, a Brussels carpet, a piano and a crew of twenty men.

The Brocklehurst boat, the Lydn (promptly rechristened the Bagstones) is smaller. In between intensive bouts of sightseeing in and around Cairo, the MBs devote their energy and interest to making it feel like home. Marianne describes ending a day's shopping 'by investing in a fine but rather crooked lamp for our saloon with which and other articles de luxe we go tumbling down the bank to our boat in the dark.'

At last all is ready and they set off on their 1000-mile voyage up to the Second Cataract. Amelia records the moment of departure:

*The awning that has all day roofed in the upper deck is taken down; the captain stands at the head of the steps; the steersman is at the helm; the dragoman has loaded his musket. Is the Bagstones ready? We wave a handkerchief of inquiry – the signal is answered – the mooring ropes are loosened – the sailors pole the boat off*

*from the bank—bang go the guns, six from the
Philae, and six from the Bagstones, and away we
go, our huge sail filling as it takes the wind [...]
We sit on the high upper deck, which is furnished
with lounge-chairs, tables and foreign rugs, like
a drawing room in the open air, and enjoy the
prospect at our ease.*

Their progress up the Nile is punctuated by
halts to explore ancient sites, 'grub' for antiquities
in the sand, picnic on Persian rugs, visit bazaars,
exchange civilities with local dignitaries, shoot,
sketch, paint—and socialise. The dahabeeyahs on
the river are constantly meeting and organising
excursions. Often they moor together at night and
there is a flurry of on-board dinner parties. For
the indomitable MBs, who soon dispense with the
services of their incompetent dragoman, Catafago,
there is also the serious business of marketing for
provisions. The two women take to bartering as to
the manner born:

*It was fine to see the Sitti sitting on a mat in the
middle of the general ash hole or grand square of
the town doing bazaar over 2 sheep, looking wise
and feeling their ribs.*

In the midst of it all, Marianne finds time to
continue her diary. Her comments on Egyptian

men, ancient and modern (as well as their European counterparts) are lively and astute:

*Tih was evidently a gentleman of humgumtion. He lived 6000 years ago, and built his own tomb and had it carved and painted in all its chambers with scenes that represented his various possessions and occupations, his farms, his beasts, his slaves and all they did, while he himself is often repeated of a considerable size, which showed his general superiority. Occasionally a very diminutive wife and children are thrown in, who did not appear to count for much.*

Hassenein, a nineteenth-century dragoman, is summed up with equal adroitness:

*Old Hassenein [...] comes on and makes love to us with a lump of sugar of which there is a scarcity. They say he has an eye upon us for Syria. Nice old fellow, very like a bit of Turkish Rhubarb.*

Though the beauty of her surroundings sometimes causes Marianne to bubble over into lyricism, what really charges her writing with energy and excitement is the feeling of danger. She gives an entertaining account of the laborious ascent of the First Cataract, but it is the return journey, when the dahabeeyahs shoot the rapids, that she finds truly exhilarating:

*We see before us a narrow passage between high granite rocks where the water is regularly roaring for about three hundred yards and with a sudden rush and a bound we are in for it. The great boat gathers fresh impetus every moment, the very Arabs forget to scream for some moments, and just at the last, when we seem to be tearing straight down upon the wall of rocks before us, the steersmen (four of them) give us a good twist and we turn sharp to the left and escape with our lives...*

With the same relish for adventure, she throws herself wholeheartedly into highly illegal, cloak-and-dagger negotiations to acquire a mummy. Though indignant about vandals who carve their names on temples, she apparently has no conscience about grave-robbing. Amelia Edwards, too, is not averse to a spot of illicit antiquity hunting:

*I may say, indeed, that our life here was one long pursuit of the pleasures of the chase. The game, it is true, was prohibited; but we enjoyed it none the less because it was illegal. Perhaps we enjoyed it the more [...] There were whispers about this time of a tomb that had been discovered on the western side — a wonderful tomb, rich in all kinds of treasures. No one of course had seen these things [...]*

> *But there was a solemn secrecy about certain of*
> *the Arabs, and a conscious look about some of the*
> *visitors, and an air of awakened vigilance about*
> *the government officials, which savoured of mys-*
> *tery [...] Dark hints were dropped of a possible*
> *papyrus; the MBs babbled of mummies; and an*
> *American dahabeeyah, lying innocently off Kar-*
> *nak, was reported to have a mummy on board.*

In fact, unknown to each other at the time, Amelia
and Marianne were rivals for the purchase of the
papyrus but, as Amelia records, the MBs

> *bought both mummy and papyrus at an enor-*
> *mous price; and then, unable to endure the per-*
> *fume of their ancient Egyptian, drowned the dear*
> *departed at the end of a week.*

(Marianne's own appended version of events,
'How We Got Our Mummy', is rather more diplo-
matic about the mummy's disposal.)

If there is a note of triumph in Amelia's account,
Marianne can crow later when the Philae travellers
have their antiquities impounded by the authori-
ties. The Brocklehursts are luckier, successfully
smuggling mummy case and papyrus aboard the
steamer at Alexandria. But this is not the end of
the trip for Marianne and Mary. Energy undimin-
ished, they have engaged a dragoman to escort

them through Palestine, Syria and the Lebanon. The party splits up, Alfred bound for Venice, the MBs for Jaffa.

Marianne and Mary continued to travel widely over the next quarter-century. Revisiting Egypt, they met Colonel Gordon, Governor of the Sudan, who took a great liking to them and called them 'the Foreign Office'. By now both were respected Egyptologists. At home, they supported the Women's Unionist Association and were vociferous anti-vivisectionists (though their fishing exploits in Ireland were frequently mentioned in *The Field*).

Over the years, Marianne had added greatly to her Egyptian collection and Emma Dent wanted to buy it for Sudeley Castle. She offered her sister £1000 but Marianne had other ideas. She was keen to build a museum in Macclesfield and in 1897 she and her brother Peter founded the West Park Museum, where the collection is still.[3]

According to scrapbooks which Marianne kept at the time, there was much disagreement with the local council over the design of the museum and this upset her greatly. She was not present at the official opening in October 1898, having broken her collarbone in a fall at her London house in Connaught Square. She died there later that month. Her obituary in the local press mentions the accident but states that 'she appeared to be progressing as favourably as could be expected [...] so that her somewhat sudden death came all the more as a surprise.'[4] Such discreet wording gives little preparation for the shock contained in Marianne's death certificate: she committed suicide. She was brought home to Cheshire for a quiet burial in a grave she herself had chosen in Wincle churchyard.[5] Mary was left Bagstones for her lifetime and, when she died in 1912, aged 82, was buried in the same grave.

A happier note to end on, and one more in keeping with Marianne's zestful life, is the picture she conjures up at the end of her diary, as she and Mary prepare for the Middle East:

*We stop all day at Port Said, we two MBs picnicking on the banks of the Suez Canal, picking up coral from the Red Sea and prowling on the shore of Lake Manzalee, where dead flamingoes lie about on the sand. A good passage we have had, and another in prospect...*

# Notes to Introduction

1 All extracts from Amelia Edwards are taken from *A Thousand Miles up the Nile* (Century Publishing, London, 1982), first published by Longmans in 1877.

2 See Jean Bray, *The Lady of Sudeley* (Long Barn Books, Ebrington, 2000). This is a biography of Emma Dent and a valuable source of information about the Brocklehurst family.

3 The collection is fully catalogued in *The Macclesfield Collection of Egyptian Antiquities* by Rosalie David (Aris & Phillips Ltd, Warminster, 1980).

4 *The Macclesfield Courier,* October 1898

5 The publishers are indebted for this and much other information relating to Marianne's life to Kate Reeder, formerly Collections and Exhibitions Officer at Macclesfield Museums Trust and now Assistant Keeper of Social History at Beamish, The North of England Open Air Museum.

# The Diary

The slim, black, leather-bound book in which Marianne Brocklehurst kept her diary of her trip to Egypt in 1873-1874 was given by her family to Macclesfield Borough Council for the Museum, where it is still a treasured possession.

In transcribing Marianne's handwriting, we have retained her erratic spellings, including her variations on names. Her punctuation, however, has been altered in the interests of easier reading and we have corrected any obvious mistakes with dates.

Marianne's pages are full of illustrations, from water-colours to witty drawings and thumbnail sketches. We have reproduced a range of them to show the appeal of the original diary.

*Tuesday, Nov. 11, 1873*

Having seen our 18 cwt of luggage off in a van
—Catafago seated at the top and George hastily
bidden from the cellars below, where at the last
moment he was having a last hasty snatch of beef
and pickles—we wound up our own little affairs
with 'jost a chope' and departed with coupons for
Brindisi, which we ever after had reason to regret.
Our night view of the sea at Dover was not cheer-
ing, but morning beheld us performing a fair passage to Calais.

1

*Wednesday, Nov. 12*

Received at Paris by the junger Herr and whilst waiting for bagages courier, B. was accosted by a splendid footman who asked if she was going to St Germain, an English lady answering her description being expected by the ancient noblesse there. Hotel du Louvre.

*Thursday, Nov. 13*

Sightseeing in Paris — ruins of the old Opera House, lately burnt down, Place Vendome, where they are re-erecting the column, the Madeleine, Place de la Concorde, Arc de Triomphe in the distance, fishing party on the Seine, the Louvre and its pictures. After dinner, a little tour en fiacre by the still ruined Hotel de Ville, Notre Dame, the Palais de Justice, not yet restored. Landed at the Palais Royal where we spent a profitable hour gazing at the diamonds and black pearls and investing to the sum of three francs in an elegant purse for Alfred. Left in the evening for Turin.

*Friday, Nov. 14*

Day dawning as we crossed the Rhone after leaving Macon, but not until towards three in the afternoon did we, by ascending through the pretty,

In the train for the Mont Cenis and were we not told 50 times "there is a glacier here is the Tunnel" and "Modane is on the Italian side"! until it was discovered she was reading her guide-book the wrong way about.

mountainous range of limestone cliffs, reach the Mont Cenis Tunnel, having been previously searched and lunched at Modane. We entered the Tunnel after a series of false alarms and tunnels of minor importance. When half way through, the descent began and, emerging rather rapidly on the Italian side, we found ourselves in the midst of fresh fallen snow. We had taken 28 minutes to get through. The descent was extremely disagreeable and shaky, from the steep inclines and constant use of the drag, for at least two more hours before we reached the plain of Turin, which we did about seven.

3

*Saturday, Nov. 15*

A damp dull day after the bright cold weather in France. Rambled about in the straight streets and into the Palazzo, where we saw the King's apartments and his armoury, which we all liked very much. Here are the presents to Victor Emmanuel, sent by the various cities after his liberation of Italie. There is also preserved the favourite horse of Charles Albert, which he rode during his campaign against the Austrians. Illuminations were preparing for the fête Cavour, troops marching with band playing and the dog of the regiment harnessed to the drum. Left at night and were at Bologna by three in the morning.

*Sunday, Nov. 16*

A fine bright frosty day. The old town looked bright and picturesque. Glad to fill our pockets with hot chesnuts* which the old women were roasting under the arcades and at the corners of the streets. Saw through the Archiginnasio, which contains some unique tombstones found 15 feet below the surface of the present Campo Santo. They are supposed to be something earlier than

*Marianne's original spellings have been retained throughout.

4

Etruscan and belong to skeletons which are also preserved here in the clay, as they were found, with beads and vases and pieces of money something like the beads in their right hands. The tombstones are sculptured over with figures more or less primitive, some very well formed. In the same collection is a bronze vase like a small bucket, with beautiful figures representing a sacrificial procession winding round. Afterwards to the picture gallery, where in a large picture of the Holy family by Francia we discovered the facsimile of the Madonna of Bagstones. The St Cecilia by Raphael and the Guidos Domenichino and Carracci need

Bologna

not be mentioned here. Alfred's portmanteau lost on the way from Turin. Officials assure us they have sent 20 telegrams in different directions to enquire after it—in 12 hours no answer. At night the opera, a new one, The Merchant of Venice. Music by Ciro Pinsuti, a little lame man who was constantly being brought in to receive acclamations, a large bow and a wreath carried on a tray by two footmen. The opera was very good on the whole, singing, acting and scenery all good, one of the prettiest we ever saw.

*Monday, Nov. 17*
Still no portmanteau. Fine cold weather, clear blue sky. More hot chesnuts required.

*Tuesday, Nov. 18*
Rambling about the town, trying to keep ourselves warm. Drawing in the Archiginnasio and driving to the Campo Santo. Portmanteau returns to its anxious owner.

*Wednesday, Nov. 19*
Left Bologna for Ancona, where we arrived about seven in the evening.

*Thursday, Nov. 20*
Windy and cold. Went to cathedral at top of the hill—San Cyriaco. Very old and fine porch, good tombs and strange old stones incised in black lines, with birds and animals &c. Another old church down in the town, near the hotel. Very good facades. More ancient than the Duomo. Bought pocket handkerchiefs for the benefit of the colds.

*Friday, Nov. 21*
Up early and off for Brindisi. Passed some pretty scenery and snow mountains in the distance — picture after picture, particularly where the rivers came down to the sea.

*Saturday, Nov. 22*
Brindisi. Boat in the harbour and round by the Lazaretto—painfully suggestive of what might be at Alexandria. Our spirits fall on finding out it is Saturday and not Sunday as we supposed. Called on Mr Grant, the Consul, who cheered us with a plan for snipe shooting and sent us to Mr Cokoto for cartridges. Were received and hospitably treated and had champagne administered to us by Mr Cokoto and his jolly friends—and some cartridges. Strolled through the market and saw some

splendid brigands—15 or 20—hanging together suspiciously. Found them very attractive and our admiration became so evident that the old capo di bande took the opportunity of getting a shilling out of us. Another delightful group we passed just after was a party of convicts in their red dresses, in chains, scavenging under the superintendence of a soldier with carbine and bayonet. Woodcocks and golden plover plentiful in the market, at 1½ fr and 1 franc.

*Sunday, Nov. 23*
A pouring wet day. No excursion into the country possible and no excitement except watching for the P&O Boat, which came in sight soon after

Gentlemen of Calabria
en route
for Suez Canal.

8

breakfast time, and watching some Italians swing a horse on board a steamer for Constantinople. Came on board the Simla at tea-time. All looking very placid and comfortable.

*Monday, Nov. 24*
After a horrid noisy night on board the Simla, we steam off at 7 a.m. Fine morning, breezy. Swell on the ocean but all passengers porting well. On deck after breakfast—Dalmatian coast, snow mountains. Black Prince on board en route for Lybian desert, with Prussian explorers.

*Tuesday, Nov. 25*
Very rough, dark and cloudy all day. Worse at night.

*Wednesday, Nov. 26*
Still rough but bright and blue. Awful rolling. Crashes at intervals. Water coming in at port-holes washes little women out of their berths. Another dismal night after the attempt at whist in the cabin and the utter discomfiture of dummy. Everybody holding on by the floor. Received comfort from Mrs Marshall, a lady bound for India. Things improve a little after midnight.

## Rough Sketches
### on board The Simla!

1st Day

2nd Day

View taken by M.B.

3rd Day.

4th and last Day.

END OF THE CARD PARTY!

saloon

Steward & Stewardess! Tumblers flying lamp smashed, & water coming in at the sky-light.

*Thursday, Nov. 27*
Light brings hope—but alas, instead of sighting Alexandria, we find we have gone a hundred miles out of our course and we see the coast of Egypt on the wrong side of the boat. Then we turn and

roll amongst the breakers for five mortal hours more. Alexandria at noon. Pilot declines to come on board, which we take as a sign that we are to be bored by Quarantine in durance vile for forty-eight hours on board the Simla. Quarantine officers presently take possession of us with much dignity and dirty clothes, wands in their hands. However, we are thankful to escape the Lazaretto and the companionship of 1800 pilgrims from Morocco bound for Mecca.

*Friday, Nov. 28*
In harbour at Alexandria. Make friends with pleasant people, the MacCallums, Miss Edwards, Miss Renshawe and others. We see mummy pits in the banks, the Khedive's Palace, top of Pompey's pillar, palm trees, and the faces of George and Catafago in a boat below, bringing us dates, bananas and fresh oranges — after which we are nearly imprisoned and chained by the leg to Arabs for throwing orange-peel overboard which might convey cholera to the boats below.

*Saturday, Nov. 29*
Great scrimmages. We land at Alexandria, get through the custom house with our new dress

11

improvers on, and behold the Egyptians — first impressions never to be forgotten of the crowds in the streets, the strange and many coloured dresses, the dark faces and white turbans, the fine stately men and veiled and mysterious women. It is almost a shock to plunge so suddenly into the Old World and its fashions which have not yet passed away. We are well lodged at Hotel Abat and presently take a drive round by Cleopatra's Needle and Pompey's Pillar, by groves of grand old date trees, many still loaded with fruit, up shocking bad roads where the dust and the joggling are not to be thought of by reason of the sunshine, the avenues of 'Eastern' trees, the strings of camels, the picturesque people, the little mosks, the weirdy burial grounds, the bright bazaars and the dahabeeiahs, which we go to see on the Canal.

*Sunday, Nov. 30*
We go by railway to Cairo. We join Miss Edwards and friend and 'find each other out'. We pass Lake Mereoti's mud villages, Bedouin encampments, see strange birds, cranes, ibises, camels ploughing, the fellah at his daily drudgery, and last, towards sunset, the Pyramids afar, then Cairo with its minarets and domes, and then again the crowd,

In the Delta

with Nubians, Arabs, Persians and even a snake charmer charming on the pavement, wisely with the fangs extracted from his twisting friends, and so to Hotel Shepheard, where we take up our abode. We spend the afternoon among the dahabeeiahs at Boulak and think we have made a hit in the Teodalinda.

*Monday, Dec. 1*
Signed the agreement with Mr Watson before the consul, or rather vice consul Mr Borg, for 3 months on the Nile and little did we think of what was coming! Went to the Bazaars and Mosk of Sultan Hassan, the finest and one of the oldest in Cairo, and to the Citadel at sunset—a fine view of Cairo and the quarries and away to the Pyramids and beyond.

*Tuesday, Dec. 2*
We go to the Pyramids of Gizeh, taking Mr Mac-

Callum with us and Cattafago. George on a donkey is lost to sight for the day by having missed the way and the bridge being closed—or rather opened—for dahabeeiahs to pass soon after we are over it. Alfred shoots an ibis, hoopoe and black kingfisher and stalks jackalls amongst the Pyramids at sunset. The moon rises full. It is a beautiful scene. Alfred made the ascent. We were content to visit the Tombs and ramble about the Sphinx with an attendant train of Arabs and do occasional bazaar while Mr MacCallum was sketching. We drive back to Cairo by moonlight. Evening in Mrs MacCallum's drawing room. Col. and Mrs Arendrop. Saphire rings and silk carpet to look at, fans and fly flappers.

*Wednesday, Dec. 3*
We go to take inventory on the dahabeeiah and find a very miserable specimen substituted for our fine Nubian Reis (captain). This we will not stand and have a great row about it at the Consulate with Watson. Nothing is settled. We go to the Museum with E. and R. It is a charming collection of Old Egyptian statues—that of Shafra,*

* Khafre

who built the Second Pyramid, most famous — mummies, gods, tablets, household goods, boats, weapons, gold and silver ornaments — bracelets of lapis lazzuli and gold particularly beautiful — and other antiquities. The wooden statue of the Shepherd Man (chief of a village, it is supposed) wonderfully life like, 6000 years old (Mariette), and the wooden statues of the King and Queen from Sakkara are quite unique and fresh, as if made yesterday. Afternoon at the bazaars. We see carpets but many of the new ones have strange wrong colours such as magenta in them. We hesitate about two long strips of secondhand Persian and see them in the MacCallum passage next day!!! At dinner we speak to Miss Wilson, who comes to our room and tells us of her trip with Sir J. Lubbock, Duff Grant, W. Greg &c. They are leaving for England.

*Thursday, Dec. 4*
Again to the Consulate. Watson is awkward. Nothing settled.

*Friday, Dec. 5*

We go to Ralph's Store and find a friend in him and help as to Watson and the dahabeeiah. He, having suffered from that rascally Maltese, is ready to lend us all assistance. Watson comes to terms: £20 down and to take the other boat, the Victoria, at 80. We don't see it! But we go to see the Dancing Dervishes instead, which the American lady says is 'deeply religious' and we are much impressed with the strength of their heads. They turn and waltz quickly for at least five minutes at a time, almost on the same spot. One little old grizzly man was doubly as quick and longer than the rest. His portrait is on the left hand of the drawing. We see a wedding party with drums and a funeral with

wailers, the Kedive in his carriage and his wives promiscuous in very thin veils (some are great beauties from Circassia) in other carriages, his son also driving about.

*Saturday, Dec. 6*
Busy ordering stores from Osman's, who is dear. We arrive on the Shoobra road, the fashionable park drive of Cairo and something less bumpy than the others. Avenues of trees of sycamore figs.

*Sunday, Dec. 7*
Church at the New Hotel well filled. At the Museum again with E. and R. and drive on the Shoobra road. 'Penelope Ann.'

*Monday, Dec. 8*
With Mr Ralph to choose another dahabeeiah. Take the Lydn. Afterwards it is rechristened the Bagstones. It has no kitchen or canteen, however!

*Tuesday, Dec. 9*
We conclude the bargain for the Lydn, £65 a month (or less?), hire canteen from Tel Hami, draggoman to the MacCallum party, for £10, deposit £20 at the Consulate and hope thereby we have got rid

17

of Watson. Do our further shoppings in the Moos-qui, shot cartridges &c, and ride donkeys to the dahabeeiah to inspect matters there.

*Wednesday, Dec. 10*
Busy about the boat. Mr Ralph very helpful. All looks cheery. The kitchen progresses.

*Thursday, Dec. 11*
Whilst M.I.B. is at the boat, I and Alfred go with E. and R. to see the procession of pilgrims starting for Mecca. Out of the great gate come camels with palanquins and camels with riders, sheiks, priests and the like, dervishes and pilgrims on foot, flags of all kinds, regiments of soldiers, horses, holy men in many coloured garbs. The fat man who rides bare-backed to Mecca is the sheik of the camels. And last, the Golden Pagoda and white camel. This contains the new and sacred carpet which every year goes to replace the other one at Mecca. We saw the Holy Sheik who on the return rides over the prostrate crowd. We saw other green turbans of the Mahomet family and were altogether greatly satisfied with this Eastern spectacle and the crowds of devotees and the faithful in general. This night we slept on our dahabeeiah and like it much. George

is the moving power. Cattafago, useful up to this point, begins to show utter incapacity.

*Friday, Dec. 12*

First day on our dahabeeiah. We begin with a great row to get off, waiting for the Reis, an antiquee of at least a hundred years, 'he waiting for the sailors' bread'. They manage to start us at last, just too late to get through the bridge. We pay the toll, £3, and feeling rather small land and walk to the Philae, which is on the other side the bridge, lunch with our friends and finish the day's shopping in Cairo by investing in a fine but rather crooked lamp for our saloon, with which and other articles de luxe we go tumbling down the bank to our boat in the dark.

our old
Reis.

*Saturday, Dec. 13*

Breakfast at Shepherds, see the MacCallum pictures of Jerusalem and Jaffa, say adieu to Cairo and at 2 o'clock set sail with a good wind, a comfortable boat and a pleasant looking lot of sailors. There is the steersman, Reis Mahommet (2nd Reis but really first in command), a Nubian of deep die, a merry excitable fellow, an excellent sailor and soon a great favourite with us all, Joseph, who talkee leetle Engliz, Fodle (virtue) a strong made Nubian, blue black, Hadji Mahommed, 'the responsible', and little Osman, surnamed Goggles, the smallest man with the biggest spirit on the boat, afterwards revered by all in his various capacities of desperate swimmer, sailor, washerwoman and dress-maker. Abdallah, the good tempered, and four others of no particular attractions, a serpenty gentleman, Cook, at £12 a month, and a melancholly man called the Marmeton, or kitchen maid, complete our crew. We have a brisk and lovely voyage to Bedri Shayn, 18 miles, where we anchor at night. The boat shows very good sailing powers and is not content with always following her large and illustrious consort. The views on each side have been beautiful, first passing picturesque old Cairo with its little mosks and date trees, always with their lovely background of limestone ridge and quarries of the Mokattene Hills, worked for stone from the Pyramids till now. On the other hand, the Pyramids of Gizeh and then the Pyramids of Sakkara, a dozen at least, standing out on the plain in ever changing variety of lights and colours, with villages, date trees, the river and pretty old boats painted up by the setting sun and afterglow into exquisite pictures.

*Sunday, Dec. 14*
We join Miss Edwards and Renshaw with donkies for a day amongst the Pyramids and Tombs of Sakara. These ladies being in sole command at present are proportionately jolly. The mutual dinner parties given and champagne that flowed need not be mentioned here. The Tomb of Tih is one of the finest and oldest in Egypt. It interested us much. The figures are so well drawn and so slim. Tih was evidently a gentleman of humgumtion. He lived 6000 years ago and built his own tomb and had it carved and painted in all its chambers with scenes that represented his various possessions and occupations, his farms, his beasts, his slaves and all they did, while he himself is often repeated of a considerable size, which showed his general

superiority. Occasionally a very diminutive wife and children are thrown in, who did not appear to count for much. After Tih, we had lunch at Mariette Bey's empty house. Mariette is now 'King Cole' in Egypt and has surveillance of the Museum and all the antiquities. His book is excellent, 'The Itineraire'. The Colossus in the Water — which puzzled George, who asked Lane, who didn't explain — is disappointing but the sunsetty ride back through Memphis by the two picturesque mud villages and under the palms when the goats and buffaloes and sheep and oxen and ploughs and fellaheen were coming home was delightful.

*Monday, Dec. 15*
Set up a tent at Memphis. Sketching, grubbing.

*Tuesday, Dec. 16*
A good wind early and away we go. Sail all day and are at Rigga at night. We pass the False Pyramid towards sunset. It is called false because built round a rock but it is supposed to be older than Gizeh and more carefully built. It has never been opened. Flocks of wild geese are seen.

*Wednesday, Dec. 17*

Again the wind favours us and we drive along to Benisooef. We pass an iron dahabeeiah stuck on a sandbank with five unfortunate ladies (Stewarts) on board. A few days after we hear that a steamer even then had failed to get them off. So much for iron on the Nile! And at the Cataracts in case of a breakage there can be no repairs for a month. We also pass the Cleopatra (Madame Georgie and Miss Berresford) with ease. This is hitting one of our own size. With the Philae, we keep up comfortably. At night, an alarm of robbers. A man swims round both boats, but is well shouted at before he can get on either, after which they make great demonstrations of catching him, in the felucca, which is a safe course. Presently I see the guard subside again into his little hole on the bank and all is over.

*Thursday, Dec. 18*

The wind has changed to the south. It is very cold, dust and wind prevail. We do bazaar in the dark and dirty little street at Benisooef, buy greens and are fussed by Cattafago. We go shooting on the other side of the river, where the 'bad men' are living in tents: wretched Arabs in one-sided erections of straw or rough covering, not to be called tents.

23

where the "bad men" live—near Benisooef.

Our sailors seem afraid of them and say all bad men here up to Assiout. We fall among sand grouse and sand partridges, which delays our return till after dark. Friends and Catty are alarmed.

*Friday, Dec. 19*
Cold S. wind, dull sky and even a little rain—a great wonder in Egypt. Boat cannot stir. Here we first saw silver torcs, as well as the everlasting bracelets and anklets on the women. Very handsome things. The Philae dines with us.

*Sunday, Dec. 21*
Get well away with a north wind. We dine with the Philae at Maghagha.

*Monday, Dec. 22*
Good wind. We get to Golossonah.

*Tuesday, Dec. 23*
Golossonah. A miserable collection of mud walls and squallid inhabitants but the pigeon palaces under the date trees are very pretty. It was fine to see the Sitti sitting on a mat in the middle of the general ash hole or grand square of the town doing bazaar over 2 sheep, looking wise and feeling their ribs. The bargain concluded by giving a napoleon apiece for them. One is a present to the sailors, who get a napoleon backsheesh at each principal town (nine of them) and an occasional sheep. Our two attendant sailors with their long sticks kept off a portion of the population, the crawling dirty

Pigeon castles at golosanah

children and filthy womenkind being the most objectionable part. Here Alfred shot beautiful little green bee-eaters. Afternoon, went on to Minieh.

*Wednesday, Dec. 24*
Bazaar at Minieh. Waiting for Mr MacCallum and Mr and Mrs Ayr.*

*Thursday, Dec. 25*
Christmas Day. Towing. We go to a state dinner on the Philae, which is illuminated with 50 lanterns. Sailors sing and dance and do fantasia, one acting a Governor. Very comic performance. All his judgments duly given to the biggest bribe, and chair of state constantly upset.

*Friday, Dec. 26*
We are unkindly bumped by the Philae and left on a sandbank. We all get to Roda at noon. Our new cook is waiting for us. Sudden dismissal of the old one, who made the sheep and beef go nowhere! This came by telegram and Mr Ralph's kind offices. Here the railway ends.

*Travelling companions who journey by train from Cairo to join Misses Edwards and Renshawe on the Philae at Minya.

*Saturday, Dec. 27*

Good wind. Pass Beni Hassan and the celebrated tombs, 'no stop' the Christian convent. Specimens of Christian monks who swim across and board us for backsheesh not prepossessing. We roast under the rocks of Gebel Aboofeyda, which are magnificent crags of limestone, full of tombs and old anchorite caves. Crocodiles here sometimes — one shot by Lord Ducie last year. A storm comes on and drives us wildly into a bend of the river near Manfaloot. Several other dahabeeiahs are also sheltering there. We go shooting when the wind abates. Sand grouse and plovers.

*Monday, Dec. 29*

Get away from the corner. A little wind, sometimes towing. A. shoots green plovers and pigeons. Anchor not far from Assiout at night.

*Tuesday, Dec. 30*

We leave the boat and go by donkeys to Assiout across country. Very pretty. Assiout lies below the mountain — minarets amongst the mud walls and mud walls amongst the bright green. A curious white domed burial ground beyond.

*Wednesday, Dec. 31*

Join forces to see the tombs in the limestone rocks of the mountain. Pretty colours and patterns of the ceilings. Lovely view. We buy fly flappers with ivory handles. Here the sailors take their 24 hours for baking. Mr MacCallum sends his whip in ceremony down to the Bakehouse towards sunset and the bread comes and we start. The bread is the one great nuisance on the boat. It is cut up in small pieces and dried in the sun on deck over one's head. As it hardens it is turned over and scrubbled about several times in the day. It is enough to drive a fellow wild. The sailors have a little kitchen fire of their own and a large pot. They soak their bread in hot water and make some kind of mess of it in a large bowl and squat round in a circle for a meal on this plain bill of fare and drop of drink out of the Nile. They seem content and strong and very good tempered.

*Thursday, Jan. 1*

Fine. A little wind. Moonlight walk on the sand — desert indeed. Punch on the Philae afterwards.

*Friday, Jan. 2*

Good wind. Anchor near Shoohag. Have had the

hills and cliffs near the river at times. Then we are sure to have gusts, and sudden ones, down the valleys. It helps the sailing but requires all to be wide awake. We like cliffs!

*Saturday, Jan. 3*
Pass the White Monastery. Little pigeon shooting first. Good wind. Rush along all day. Pass Girgeh.

*Sunday, Jan. 4*
Kasr-es-Said. No wind, hot walking. Beautiful view of rocky hills, mosk, plain, camels, village and curious new style of pigeon towers. The pigeons in Egypt are of more consequence than the natives. They always inhabit the upper stories which are variously architectured to please their tastes and elegantly painted in stripes and stuck round with sticks for their further convenience in alighting. And yet the birds are not valued beyond their agricultural importance in the manuring line. The Hawagha may kill 30 or 40 anywhere and very good in the pot we find them and no one cares much about it. We see them by thousands living famously on the indian corn and durra of which the Egyptians make their bread, no one objecting in the least. Mr Unwin has the 'awful luck' of get-

ting a shot at a crocodile here. Nobody else sees one. Our 3 dahabeeiahs together.

*Monday, Jan. 5*
Towing all day.

*Tuesday, Jan 6*
Ditto, but we all walk to the Temple of Denderah, our first temple, and are very much impressed, not so much with the outside which looks flat, half hid with sand and of the Egyptic shape, which we don't like, but with the grand figures and massive pillars in the great gloomy hall, the pillars and walls of which—and of the corridors and side chapels—are carved with hieroglyphics and scenes representing the King, triumphant over his enemies, entering with offerings and received by various gods into the temple and conducted by them further into the adytum, the holiest place, where he alone is permitted to look upon the most sacred symbol, in this case the sistrum, the emblem of Isis. All the temples, according to Marriette, were built not for religious use for the people but simply as a token of homage from the King to the gods who had given him victory, or whom he wished to please. The procession of King

and priests, as it passed through the various halls and chambers and ascended to the roof in view of the people outside, is in this temple curiously represented everywhere, even on the walls of the staircase. Denderah has its roof on and is the most perfect temple left in Egypt, having been buried in sand and dug out again, but it is only a little more than 2000 years old! and consequently regarded as quite a parvenu, and right minded critics tell you it is overdone with hieroglyphics and figures. This did not appear to our admiring and astonished gaze! Cleopatra's portrait is somewhere on the walls. Walking back in the dark, two or three miles, was a matter of stumbling, till shots were fired and lanterns appeared from the dahabeeiahs at their new moorings!

*Wednesday, Jan. 7*
Good wind to Keneh. We have to stop to buy charcoal and dates. Here we first saw Ghawarghee, the dancing girls of Egypt. Ride donkeys to tour town, 3 miles, and quarrel—with old Catty, as usual, always wrong. The other dahabeeiahs go on. We follow.

*Thursday, Jan. 8*

The Cleopatra comes up. A. shoots a duck. Miss Berresford comes on board to see our birds.

*Friday, Jan. 9*

We see the Philae early in the morning, tow and sail after her to Luxor. Land and call for letters at the Consul's house. It is a picture in itself, built into the temple with a pretty doorway and coloured all to harmonize. Mustapha Agha is a very old gentleman, very polite and pleasant for an old Turk. We ride on to Karnac, past the grand obelisk of Luxor and the two collossi of Rameses at the gate, 2 miles to Karnac, once joined by avenues of sphinxes and temples. We spend the afternoon among Karnac's immense halls and gorgeous ruins. It is very

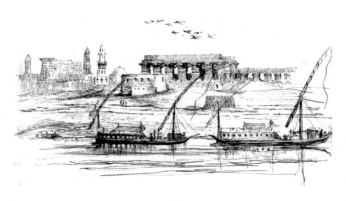

splendid. Alfred shoots a fox and thinks more of it than the temples, naturally. Return to coffee at Mustapha Agha's and do a little dealing 'under the rose'. The Cleopatra ladies are kind to us about some money. A high wind and storm of sand at night.

*Saturday, Jan. 10*
A morning call on old Mustapha, and pipes. Wind is still high. We go again to Karnac, meet the Cleopatra ladies. Pleasant chat. Another fox slain. Consul and Governor, his son, dine with us. Much secret conference over antiquities. Old fox. Miss my magnifier afterwards! Philae and Mansoura go off. We have it out with Cattafago.

*Sunday, Jan. 11*
A good morning's work done in getting rid of poor old Catty, who may now go to his 'high familee in Seeria'. Out of his place here, always spying, useless, unhappy, expensive and anything but a luxury. It must be a mutual relief. How we enjoy our freedom afterwards and to be on 'the Nile without a dragoman' is heavenly and worth the little extra bother we have had ten times over. Sailors in great good humour at the compliment the Sitti pay them

and away we go. Catch up the Philae in two hours and are at Erment at sunset.

*Monday, Jan. 12*
A wind. The Fostat comes up and races the Philae. We are first into Esneh. Pretty place, horrible looking people and dancing girls. We bazaar on our own account with Joseph's assistance. Buy geese, turkeys, chickens, eggs, sheep, all in odd quantities and up very odd streets. M.I.B. smokes a pipe over the oil can and is very proud of her bargains. For £5.0.0., 300 eggs, 38 chickens, 4 geese, 2 sheep, half a cow and vegetables. This with our present store will provision us for a month, which is necessary as after Assouan we may expect to get nothing much in Nubia but castor oil. The temple of Esneh is fine, though half buried in the sand and newly excavated. The interior is rather dark, with beautiful columns well sculptured and with grand capitals. It is not one of the very old ones, however. Miss Edwards made a very good picture of it.

*Tuesday, Jan. 13*
At Esneh. All this time the days have been generally bright but cold, the nights very cold (the thermometer about 50 to 60). We have sometimes resolved

to write a book contradicting everything that everybody has ever said about the heat, and the light clothes and the white boots requisite, and about the awful insects of which we have seen none, save a large spider or two, very alarming to the Sitti! No fleas or heavies! A mosquito or two in the cabin at night when we have neglected our net barricades has left a mark upon us. But, for the rest, Egypt of all countries we have travelled in seems singularly free from plagues of this sort.

Many nights the sailors have given us the benefit of music, tum tumty tum on the darrabukha and tambourine, the men sitting on the ground in a circle. One gets inspired at last and leads off in a high pitched voice, minor key, and after a few twists and twirls the chorus comes, a long sentimental groan of ha-a-a-ah. They sing a good deal about Lil, the night, the delightful Lil, when music begins all work is over, and about Bibi the beloved (that dirty Bibi it does not do to contemplate). They will sing for hours when once set a-going and some of their odd tunes sound quite 'Gregorian' and are quite pretty. Difficult to catch. We are constantly singing one which this party has achieved to its great satisfaction.

*Wednesday, Jan. 14*
Wind and weather permitting, we see the temple
of Edfou not far from the bank about sunset, after

a walk to a village where we bought 100 eggs and Alfred shot some pigeons. A sharp wind takes us along all night past Silsilis, where the rocks and strong currents are dangerous. 48 miles.

*Thursday, Jan. 15*
Still racing and chasing with the Philae and Fostat into Assouan but just at the last we stick on a sand bank in a high wind and cannot get off till the Philae sends some natives to our assistance. The scenery here is quite changed. Great granite rocks are piled up on each side the river and form an island, Elephantine, in the middle. We pass it on the right as we enter into the bend for Assouan. It is very curious and pretty here. We first see the deep golden, almost orange sands and sand drifts of Nubia, contrasting with the dark granite rocks very strangely. We go to bazaar in Assouan, buy curious Nubian baskets, spears, 'Madame Nubia', as they call the peculiar fringe worn by the girls but not by the women now and which constitutes full dress with bracelets and another fringe attached to silver ear-rings for the head, a Kohl bag, ostrich feathers, antelope horns and other savage articles. We hold palaver with the handsome Governor under the sycamore tree and smoke with him and

*watering the Bazaar at Assouan.*

present our letter of introduction and receive permission to go up the Cattaract in due time.

*Friday, Jan. 16*

Miss E. comes in to draw. Tel Hami brings the Reises of the other boats into our saloon, the Governor being with us, to arrange for the boats to go up. We think it cool. Much lemonade consumed and tobacco. We pay £9 to the Sheik of the Cattaract, who is to bring men and ropes sufficient for the grand pull the next day. Afterwards in the felucca amongst the islands and we land in a desolate valley by a ruined Saracenic convent and fortress to wait for jackal, which alas come not. It is a wild and strange view. Assouan lies prettily in the distance, the desert all round. The desert now has nearly all its own way and Egypt we have left and Nubia, which begins, is but a strip of vegetation half a mile broad on either side of its mother the Nile.

*Saturday, Jan. 17*
We all start from Assouan at nine, sail up the river a mile or two by the islands and rocks — granite rocks which are heaped up on either side and remind us of Cornwall and Scilly. Some have hieroglyphics cut on them, cartouches (that is, ovals containing the name of a king) shewing that their majesties went up the Cataract, or did not go up, as it happened. On arriving at the first bab or gate of the Cataract, we find a heavy strong current flowing over dangerous rocks and we do not find the 300 men promised by the sheik ready for us, so for these gentlemen we have to wait an hour or two. Mr MacCallum waxing wrath takes to sketching by way of cooling himself. The doctor from Sir J. Colquhoun's boat comes to Mr Ewing's to see their poor young dragoman, who has an abscess in the knee, and he pronounces it a bad case. At last

the Philae, which is first, gets into tow and a pretty row there is. Most of the Arabs scream, everybody directs, a great many look on and a few pull at the ropes, which are cleverly arranged on both sides the dahabeeiah, as well as the chief rope in front, a breakage being dangerous work amongst these sharp rocks and rushing water. After a bit, the great ship struggles up and it is our turn next, and then the Mansoura's. All manage to get up the Bab and a few hundred yards further, our boats swarming with these dirty Arabs who have us in possession. And then, though the wind is good and it is broad daylight, these doughty Arabs strike work for the day. There is nothing for it but to take a walk to the pretty village of Mahatta, half way to Philae, and Philae, the object of our desire, is but five miles from Assouan and we are likely to be three or four days getting there!

*Sunday, Jan. 18*
2nd day of cataract. Men come later than expected. More row. Another bab or so is accomplished. At 3, all declare the wind is bad and strike again.

*Monday, Jan. 19*
At last the Philae gets tugged up the Great Bab,

after breaking her rope once and nearly getting smashed. We all do the same thing, barring the breakage, and anchor soon after.

*Tuesday, Jan. 20*
4th day. At 12 o'clock the whole thing is over and the row about backsheesh begins. Our old Reis and Mohammed won't give more than the guinea agreed for and after some shoving they get rid of the last of our charming assistants and we are ourselves again. We require a good deal of cleaning up and we anchor under the beautiful little temple of Isis at Philae for the purpose. Here Mrs Lacon,

we anchor at Philae

floating down in the Peri, discovers us, stops her peri and spends the afternoon with us. We stroll about the temples afterwards until the young moon is up. This is a lovely place.

*Wednesday, Jan. 21*
Towed across the river — all are cross in consequence. No wind and no temple. Natives hold bazaar with us and here we first find the genuine Nubian lady, who smells of castor oil and has her hair in little plaits like the old Egyptian hieroglyphics, each little plait glittering with oil. The air is full of castor oil: you may scent the natives yards off! They are not pleasant to do bazaar with but mighty curious to behold, so utterly savage and strange. They wear plenty of garments, however, except the children and girls. The men are a mixture. Some are very black and their profiles have that exquisite projection of the chin before the nose which bulldogs rejoice in. Nearly all are fine made men, strong and supple. In the evening after this hot day (then 81 in the saloon) we row across to look at the beautiful sand-drift Mr Mac-Callum has fallen in love with, and whose portrait he afterwards paints so successfully, and we get a wild and curious view of the tops of the desert

hills stretching away into the distance. We pass a little mosk and a burial ground, little stones stuck up, hardly distinguishable from the desert stones which are naturally there.

*Friday, Jan. 23*
Sail all day. 50 miles. Evening, Old Hassenein (Sir J. C.'s dragoman off the Alice) comes on and makes love to us with a lump of sugar, of which there is a scarcity. They say he has an eye upon us for Syria. Nice old fellow, very like a bit of Turkish Rhubarb. Nubia, we all agree, is charming, much more beautiful than Egypt. Its dark rocky hills, sandstone, are of most fantastic shapes, sometimes so like the Pyramids we cannot believe them natural hills and we feel sure the old Egyptians got the idea of the shape from them, and the sand-drifts are exquisite, always the same glowing gold colour. The narrow border of green by the river is emerald green, though we have seen already a little barley almost ripe, and the palms and the Dom date, a lower, more spreading tree, are fine and handsome fellows. We enjoy it all immensely.

*Saturday, Jan. 24*
Sailing and towing. The cook and his kitchen maid

*Hassanein the Mediator*

fall out. Old H. comes to mediate... All is serene again. The poor d[ragoman] has the abscess cut. We call on the Philae and see McCallum's beautiful drawings. Ewings dine with us. Very jolly little people.

*Sunday, Jan. 25*
All four dahabeeiahs together. This is society on the Nile. We are a pretty sight. It is cheerful and about 60 miles up from Philae.

*Monday, Jan. 26*
A fair wind. We keep in front all day. The scenery continues lovely. Neither pen nor pencil could

paint the warm golden soft shapely waves of sand, the beautiful forms of hills and rocks that push out from beneath, the lovely bends of river where the purple cliffs come down almost perpendicular and the blue hills melt away in the distance, the bright green line and the date and mimosa trees on the banks, everywhere where wanted. A warm mild sunny day, yet at noon a gust of wind unexpectedly catches us all, cracks one cross mast at top (though we don't find it out till night), rips the small sail of the Philae in two, off and breaks off the top of the cross mast of the Alice entirely. The Fostat in the distance is never seen again and we don't know what damage she did not sustain. Anchor near Korrosco. Head wind. Here should be crocodiles. Accordingly we hear wonderful tales about them, some unknown person has just shot 4, 7, 11, any number you like. We see a dahabeeiah go down with two hanging on the cross pole. Things begin to shape themselves. It is Mr Grantly Berkeley who has been doing it and is now up the river in a punt, waiting for several dead bodies to come up.

*Tuesday, Jan. 27*
We have our first ride on camels. It is not so bad, only the jerk coming down again is tremendous.

Walking, we see white hawks. The Ewings see a tortoise and a crocodile. Too bad of them!

*Wednesday, Jan. 28*
Still trying to tow over these long 12 miles from Korrosco to Der, the rocks and stones in the river and the head wind being frightful impediments. Here we have some bad legs on hand, several stomach aches in which Essence of Ginger plays a prominent part and is much respected. Foddle, with an incipient sunstroke, is roasting his head over the fire and has to be removed into the small boat and played upon with water from the Nile,

out of a can. A cup of tea completes his cure, while Hadji Mohammed requires two, and a piece of plaster to his toe, likewise for sunstroke and cut to his foot combined. Rather a severe case! It is tiring work for the poor fellows who are not sustained as we are by the beauty of the scenery! Temple of Amada is a very nice little temple, full of good figures on the walls and pillars. We creep in and out over the sand-drifts at the door. American party comes up. Fat dragoman eyes us with a hope for the future, as a butcher would a lamb, and is glad to hear we've got rid of the Syrian gentleman and that 'dam bad cook'.

after a hard days towing.

*Thursday, Jan. 29*

We get to Der, capital of Nubia, a cleaner, nicer little town than we have seen. The ladies are rather grand in their draggletails and more castor oily than ever. Here the temple is cut in the rock, the first we have seen. Very old and rather rough and delapidated, but interesting, the figures large. Four must have stood outside and four have sat in the sanctuary, two or three times larger than life. The new graves outside are covered with pebbles and a bowl of water at the foot of each is replenished by the relatives. We wondered with what idea? The sheikh's house and sword rather grand. The doors of many houses were ornamented, one very fine with a willow pattern soup-plate let into the mud over the top! Tea on the Mansoura. Narrow escape of Mrs E.'s head from the iron support that gave way. Monkeys &c.

*Friday, Jan. 30*

Sailing slowly. We coffee and 'kef' under a grand old mimosa tree on the bank with the E.s. Here was a grave of a village sheik. On the tree, pots of incense and a little copper bell, underneath, a small canoe in straw, while a sealed pot of money stood by the grave. The ground was black and charred where the sheep had been roasted and eaten to his memory or for the benefit of his soul, which doubtless is expected to ring the bell if it wants anything more than the canoe to travel in, the money to pay the fare, the sheep to live upon and the incense to precede it into the next world and let them know it is coming. At least, so we take it! We go to see the curios on the Alice and to help to mend the broken wing of the hawk on the Philae. The Philae dine with us and afterwards all the boats' crews come pouring in to see the 'Hawagha Gorg' performing the Arab dance with all its wriggles, to the sound of the tumtum and tamborine, and dressed in proper Arab togs! Dancing continues to a late hour, Foddle succeeding 'Gorg' and a mad fellow off the Alice finishing off.

*Saturday, Jan. 31*
A fair sailing day. We have a scramble along the rough banks and feel for our own little chaps who have pulled us along over so many miles of them. Tea on the M. Doctor thinks their poor dragoman getting worse. We supply a bottle of port which we hear afterwards he won't take, having religious scruples against wine and meat, the only things that might save him. It is a bad case indeed. It seems

he has had himself bled at nearly every town and thinks that if this and fasting and a row of amulets round his neck with bits of the Koran in them won't cure him, it is Allah's will that he should die and he prefers to accept it. The steersman also is a dervish and possesses an amulet with a bigger bit of the Koran in it and he sits all day with the sick man and they have the big amulet out and feel better, though they can neither of them read a word of it. The round sugar loaf hills are very curious about here and so are the perfectly round sand banks like inverted basins. They want looking into!

*Sunday, Feb. 1*
We get to Abooseer at night. The moon is bright and we see the great figures of the temple plain

50

enough a mile away. We land and struggle up the bank to the sand drift which once hid all, until Belzoni and others cleared it on one side and brought to light the temple and the grand gigantic statues sitting on each side the door, as they have sat for 6000 years or so: four statues of King Rameses, each 70 feet high. One is fallen, the others very perfect, even the faces. Smaller figures, which reach only to their knees, would make decent statues anywhere else. The hall of the temple cut in the rock is supported by 16 figures of Osiris, 18 feet high. It leads into a sanctuary where four sitting statues are by the altar. Other chambers in the rock are all covered with bas reliefs of battles and chariots, the arks carried by the Egyptians into foreign countries and other curious subjects, very large and well executed, full of spirit. A good deal of colour is left on them. Faces all handsome and mild in expression. We were immensely impressed and think it the finest thing we have seen in the world. I suppose there is no temple so old or so grand anywhere.

*Monday, Feb. 2*
We go on, leaving the Philae to paint pictures. The Mansoura and Alice follow later in the day. The

scenery is still very beautiful and curious, the hills such odd shapes. May sugar loafs look like little extinct volcanoes? Sand banks are closely watched for Themsa. At last M.B. calls out for A.B. There are two large black and white geese with a log in front of them A.B. thinks will just do to creep behind. He flies for his gun. Meantime the Sitti keep watch. M.B. says to M.I.B., passing the glasses, 'I am not sure about that log,' and while they gaze the log gets up and walks deliberately into the water, displaying four legs and a tail and all of an olive green colour. Oh!!! The geese don't wait. Another crocodile is seen on the same bank. The Mansoura joins us at night. The poor dragoman is worse.

We tow a bit and stop and walk with Mrs E. and get pebbles on the shore. This is a good part for pebbles. Mr E. and Alfred go in their felucca to shoot crocodiles. Moreover they shoot one! A. describes how it lay asleep in the sun on a flat sand bank. They, dropping quietly downstream upon it, got within 50 yards. Mr E., with his Express resting on the boat, fired and they think hit him under the shoulder as the beast stood on his head, turned over and then lashed his tail from one side to the other and plunged into the water. It remains to be proved by him coming up again—a matter of

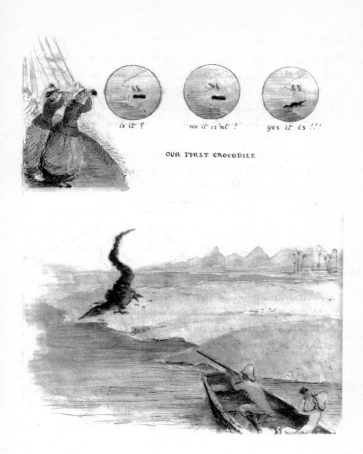

is it ?  no it is'nt !  yes it is !!!

OUR FIRST CROCODILE

perhaps six days. Notice is given to the natives to look out for him and plenty backsheesh promised if found! M.B. has toothache.

*Tuesday, Feb. 3*

We sail again, Alice first. All see one large crocodile on a sandbank about a hundred yards from
the boat. We think he came back each time after
the dahabeeiahs passed. Mr Ewing stops and
waits for him in a hole he scratches in the sand but
Mr Themsa does not come up for the fourth time
of asking and Mr Ewing's 'backbone is melted' to
no purpose. Wady Halfeh is rather a dreary place
except for the bales of merchandize the caravans
have brought and left in heaps on the shore, each
pile a separate affair, having been brought from the
interior (Soudan) to be taken on by boat to Cairo or
vice versa. They look very picturesque, with a fire
sometimes, and a tent, and wild looking fellows all
round. Mansoura comes up.

*Wednesday, Feb. 4*

Three feluccas sail up to the Rock of Abouseer.
We scramble up through the deep sand and have
a fine view of the cataracts and rocks, a strange lot
of little islands of sand and lumps of black, highly
polished granite which we have just passed. The
rapids are not so strong as at the 1st Cataract, but
shallower. No dahabeeiah can get up. Everything
goes on by camels. Dongola is a four days' ride

from here. Unfortunately, the wind was high and the air full of sand and we could not see much of the distant view to the hills above Dongola which we ought to have done. This is a grand rock, 200 feet above the river, and to quote Mr Murray is 'the Ultima Thule of most Nile voyagers'. It has names of the illustrious cut all over it. We saw Peytherick, Tatton Sykes, F. W. Holland amongst the rest. This is all very well here but it is abominable to disfigure the temples and tombs and we were grieved to see great name of Murray itself confronting us largely on the grand figure, the first as you enter the Temple of Abou Simbel. We had a rough hard pull back again (5 miles) and a dangerous crossing of the river at last, the waves and wind high against us. But Foddle's spirit and Said's rose to the emergency, while faithful Yosef's and Abdallah's faces were long and anxious. Another boat and the rest of our sailors put out to meet us but fortunately we did not need them as our new pilot steered us well over, head up the stream. Very rough night again. Rudder makes a desperate noise and drives us into the saloon with our blankets. A.B. is poorly.

*Thursday, Feb. 5*
A native hunter appears on the scene, ready to go

Etmann.
Syad e Timsāh.
Aousaib.

up to the Cataracts and shoot crocodiles and A.B. is much better at once. We start them off, George and sailors. They afterwards report too windy for many crocodiles but they got very near one big fellow who, however, was off like a shot before a shot could be fired. A. killed a fine goose but lost it at last. Hopes for better luck next time. The old hunter is a fine old specimen. Meantime we saw our Mansoura friends again and picked up pebbles at all spare moments and tried to do bazaar and flew on shore when Yosef announced 'five teen gemel go to Soudan whole man stop here', by which we knew that a caravan had arrived from Soudan and this now was our chance. The five teen camels certainly lay resting on the ground and very nice they looked, but their packages contained nothing but Gum Arabic and fond as the writer is of her gum bottle it was still a little trying to find nothing else to bazaar about. The dark gentlemen belonging to the bales seemed quite sorry for our disappointment and offered to sell us one of themselves, a very tall savage of quite the Albert Nyanza cut! He also recommended himself and showed us how he could carry a good weight, pronounced himself equal to carrying the Sitti both at once anywhere, with other qualifications. But, his price being fixed at £100, he was considered rather too dear.

*Saturday, Feb. 7*
Very windy and very cold. Mansoura and Alice get off early but not far. Wind against them.

*Sunday, Feb. 8*
Alfred and the syad go again to the Cataract but it is so cold no crocodiles are out. A. kills a large white vulture which was feasting with two others on a dead donkey. A select dinner party. The Philae arrives. They all go up to Abou Seer. Very windy night and very cold. Meantime, to quote Murray, 'the big yard and sail have been taken down and

fastened above the deck, and the small one hoisted on the main mast. The oars are out and some of the planks taken up to make room for the rowers' legs.' So our Bagstones has lost much of her beauty and some of her inmates are right sorry they are at their journey's end. One was heard to remark, 'he wished they were going another thousand miles up the Nile', which was at all events a compliment to all concerned.

*Monday, Feb. 9*
We turn our backs on Wady Halfeh with many regrets, in spite of having had no luck in crocodiles and dreadfully cold weather instead (the tropics are considered by this party to be 'all bosch'). The Philae is again our companion de voyage and we 'proceed', sometimes floating broadside down the river, sometimes when the wind is not against us the men row, singing lustily to help to keep in stroke. It is a new sight and very odd. The sailors are in white garments, thin and cool. A few striped waistcoats and turbans tied up with a bit of col-oured handkerchief make them into a nice picture. Somebody says 'Galley Slaves'! 24 miles this day and then we anchor. Mr MacCallum comes and fetches us on to his boat in the evening.

*Tuesday, Feb. 10*

Wind strong against us. Can't go far. Make a little way after sunset. Walked along the bank and a little way inland, where we had a very beautiful and very strange wild view of the desert which is here like a sea of sand, the hills beyond like islands, bare rocks of a lovely colour and of all sorts of shapes, pyramids, sugar loafs, and inverted pie-dishes, the foreground, curious hillocks of sand, brown with the decayed roots of the tamarisk which grew on their tops in lovely bushes, feathery and some quite grey, powdered over with white, like rime — we suppose another kind of tamarisk — excessively pretty. Brought a large branch home for the pet camelion, who expressed himself extremely gratified by immediately walking up to the topmost twig, turning himself into exactly the same colour and wearing a benignant smile for the rest of the day. This little friend (a present from the Alice) has been with us a week or more. He seems well and

happy on an allowance of 3 flies a day which have to be popped into his mouth when his indignation causes him to open it very wide and swear loudly. He also takes his drops of drink out of a silver spoon and opens his mouth for this purpose of his own accord. His colours vary from all sorts of dirty hues to a very beautiful emerald green with black stripes and spots. This, his best coat, is generally on when he is in his worst temper. It is very curious to see how nearly white he becomes against the white wall on a little iron rod over the window which is a favorite perch. His eyes, little black specs on little green lumps which he can move all round, seem capable of seeing two ways at once. He can keep an eye upon you in front at the same time he watches a fly walking up his tail at the back. A useful tail too, he twists two or three times round a doubtful perch, while feeling about with his hands (they are like a baby's glove) before taking up a new position. We hope our little friend may be spared to swear at us for many days to come.

*Wednesday, Feb. 11*
A strong cold north wind blowing dead against us! What luck! Always north when we want it

south and always south when we want it north!
Shooting quail in the afternoon. We see a dozen or
two amongst the barley and beans. The barley is in
the ear but still green. A large village under date
trees between the green strip and the desert was
very picturesque but the whole population in procession unfortunately took a deep interest in the
shooting! We bought some chickens here. After
sunset sailors rowed eight miles to Abou Simbel.
Good fellows. A bit of baccy all round.

*Wednesday, Feb. 11**
It takes 2 hours to row the dahabeeiah a mile across
to Abou Simbel. We anchor below the smaller
temple. Three other dahabeeiahs are here: Fostat,
Daphne, Philae. See the temple again and go over
in felucca to Ferhag, shoot quail, dine on the Philae.

*Thursday, Feb. 12*
Wind still against us. Miss Edwards comes on
board to sketch. We go over the smaller temple,
which is also cut in the rock and has six great figures cut in niches by the door, forming a strange

* Two separate entries for Wednesday, Feb. 11

facade out of the solid rock. Inside the hall the pillars have cats' heads for capitals and the usual ideas of kings and gods and triumphs and sacrifices, or rather offerings, are carried out in the bold fine figures sculptured on the walls. We see Mr MacCallum's fine picture of the Great Temple and have a walk with him and Miss Renshaw amongst the rocks and hills and on the yellow sand. Beautiful place.

*Friday, Feb. 13*
We start at peep o' day and in spite of wind and weather float down stream about 10 miles. Send a note by a passing dahabeeiah to Mr McC., anchor on the west side of the river. From here for the third or fourth time, we get a grand sight of the Southern Cross at three in the morning. As it rises at one and sets at four, travellers must look alive in the dead of night if they intend to see this sign in the heavens of their approach towards the other end of this world. It is a pretty constellation. Three of the stars are larger than the other and a little star has slipt on one side, where it had not ought to be, its proper place being evidently in the middle where there is none.

*Saturday, Feb. 14*

Make very little way. At evening we are near the village of Forgundi, east bank, where Alfred and M.B. go to shoot quail. They light on a native sportsman just at dusk, who says 'Gazalle Kateer' not far off, and away goes Alfred with him. They are soon lost sight of up a gorge in the rocks in the desert. Yosef and M.B. to the dahabeeiah, which has meantime made a start. They miss the felucca and have a two miles run to catch it. Turn the d. back again when A. and the syad arrive. They report having seen several gazelle, hares and a hyena. We agree to wait till next morning that they may have another turn at it, when they see some deer, gazelles and hares but all too far off to shoot.

*Sunday, Feb. 15*

We float away, sometimes rowing. It is hot and pleasant. About 3 o'clock the cry is 'temsah' and lo, three great monsters reposing on the sand some 500 yards off. A. and G. and Yosef go off in the felucca but the giants won't wait and their afternoon nap is slightly disturbed by the sudden view of a white face and a long barrel a hundred yards off and they glide into security before any shot can be fired from the bobbing felucca. Soon after we all land and see a young gazelle playing with some goats. They all belonged to some men at a shadoof. A very pretty sunset.

*Monday, Feb. 16*
Rowing today. All in good spirits. No wind, warm, sunny, delightful, very pretty. At about eleven we sight three large crocodile, stop the dahabeeiah and man the felucca, Alfred to the fore with rifle in rest, George and Mahomet rowing, Miss Booth directing with fieldglass and M.B. steering. One lovely monster glides into the water but another, equally fearful, is asleep on the end of a narrow strip of sand bank which runs half across the river. The rowers stop rowing, all sit down in the bottom of the boat, which is steered gently towards

*The 1st shot at him.*

stalking him for the second.

the sleeping beauty, who opens an eye when we are a hundred yards or so from him and makes a long neck, raising his head. At this critical moment Alfred fires. The monster gives himself a terrific shake. He is hit in the neck (one of the fatal spots). He glides slowly into the water and the family gasp and look at one another and can't believe it! Council is held. We drop a little further down the stream. Presently there is a shout from the sailors on the dahabeeiah that the crocodile is up again, hard hit. He is seen floating for some minutes and then slowly crawls up his bank again. We land the Hawagha and his trusties, the Sitti remain in the boat, the others stalk in attitudes indescribable.

'Shoot, shoot,' cries Mahomet, his little black tuft quivering again lest that lump of a crocodile should move off too soon. Crack bang. He is hit again! This time below the shoulder in his side. Again he slips into the water. The people are shouting on the other side. We watch anxiously. The beast is seen floating again, up and down, for a quarter of an hour. He disappears. Mahomet discovers him. He has sneaked up to his bank again. Again they stalk for another shot and look more ridiculous than ever. This time it is a long shot with a shaky arm and goes over his back and the poor reptile gets up and into the water again and is seen no more alive. They all say he is mortally wounded and must soon die and we are well agreed to wait three days to recover the body, which we hope to

*The last we see of him.*

exhibit as our chief trophy on the Nile. We hang about the sand bank all afternoon and see four more crocodiles. Give it up after five o'clock, when Alfred goes with his gun after some wild geese and with a return of his 'usual luck', as he says, does not get a shot at them, but tumbles onto another crocodile, so fast asleep that he and George walk through some shallow water to within 60 yards of him, fire the gun, when doubtless the shot rattling against his armour would wake him unpleasantly but without harm, and off he goes into the water, none the worse of course!

Nor does end our eventful day: we must needs have a grand row about the black butcher who kills a little cow for our benefit and walks off with the head and the cook's knife for his own. There is a fearful amount of loud talking on and off the boat, our sailors get out their long sticks, even old Reis Embarrak, and he administers it too, across the backs of three stalwart Ethiopeans who are shoved up the plank onto the boat as prisoners until the sheik of the village arrives. He brings his executioner and judgment being given against them they receive bastinado in turns, three strokes on the back, culprit lying on his stomach. The head and knife are also returned and after coffee and

Summary Justice.

pipes to the governor, all is halas. Alfred, walking in the beans in the dusk, meets a jackall and takes him for a dog until he sees his ears and tail, and then a parting shot is too late to stop his progress into the desert again.

*Tuesday, Feb. 17*
Ibreem. N. wind. We haunt the fatal bank in the felucca. Natives and sailors attempt various fishings for the crocodile in vain. We hear from shadoof man he was seen at dawn attempting to crawl on land but unable to do so. All day we are kept alive with reports of somebody who fancies he's seen

something. A. shoots 9 pigeons. Music and dancing at night, though the sailors' bread is run out to two days' store. They trust in providence and the Sitti.

*Wednesday, Feb. 18*
In the afternoon we make a drag with rope over the supposed spot where crocodile lies dead but in vain. Pick up shells. Foddle comes out as a great actor.

*Thursday, Feb. 19*
We see two crocodiles on the bank. Both jump into the water with a great splash when A. comes in view, so we hope as the third is still missing that he is dead. Go round the rocks in felucca and scramble up to Ibreem, a ruined old town once a Roman fortress. A good deal of strong Roman masonry and some granite pillars remain and a ruined church, Christian with saracenic arches and crosses. Fine view from the summit. Evening, we walk through the village of Gnaan. It is very pretty under the date trees and half built with mud, as usual, into the rocks. We find Nubian slaves here are plentiful. One girl was offered us for 70 dollars. Josef said 't' much'. The ladies who possess

these treasures look nearly as poor and dirty as the slaves but are good looking women and have fine black old Egyptian shaped eyes.

*Friday, Feb. 20*
In the afternoon a crocodile is seen floating. Everybody goes more or less mad thinking it is our particular, but it sinks and swims away at last and we are none the nearer. The Philae comes at night. We find our friends very full of a discovery made at Abu Simbel by Mr MacCallum of a painted chamber, blocked up with sand, which they got cleared away and found figures and hieroglyphics in excellent preservation, King Rameses of a very dark red and Osiris black.

*Saturday, Feb. 21*
A day of heat and suspense. Alfred shot three warran and waited for great vultures which had formed a close attachment to a dead donkey, which dead donkey when first seen in the distance we fondly hoped might be our crocodile.

*Sunday, Feb. 22*
More heat and suspense. Nothing comes of it. The people of the village are very bad fellows and

won't sell a little wheat and doura to our sailors except at an extravagant price. They get some further away and anathematize Gnaan. George kills an enormous vulture.

*Monday, Feb. 23*
We say adieu to Ibreem.

*Tuesday, Feb. 24*
We get to Korrosko. The Governor pays us a state visit, attended by the postmaster and telegraph gentleman, also the little stout jolly old sheik of the town. The visit lasts three hours. We entertain our visitors with cigars and coffee and a few words of Arabic and get very sick of them. The Governor

we approach Korosco.

presents us with sugar and charcoal. We return the compliment in 2 bottles of champagne and 2 of beer. He declines to drink before company but at sunset goes down on his knees and says some very long prayers on deck, afterwards accepting our present, which he will enjoy on the sly at home.

*Wednesday, Feb. 25*
We stay at Korrosko while Mahomet rides back to Ibreem to enquire after the crocodile. He returns late with no news of him, but a letter from the sheik, we believe, is to the effect that if found he will be forwarded. We walk amongst the mountains on the high road to Kartoum, which is no road at all but a widish valey of sand between the rocky hills, not a blade of vegetation of any kind. Dead camels, live vultures, footmarks of gazelle and the long trail of a snake was all we saw. Returned by moonlight. A German from Leipzig, Dr Jorg, called in the evening from the dahabeeiah next door. Korrosco is very pretty on its banks and the hills are lovely beyond. The booths of matting above and the mud houses on the plain of the desert and the horrible screaming women we bought beads from found us occupation.

*The Philae*

*Pigeon houses*

*The shadoof*

*Off to shoot quail*

*River scene*

*The First Cataract*

*Der*

*We do bazaar and buy a sheep*

*Temple at Abu Simbel*

*Rocks*

*Gnaan*

*The Ramesseum*

*Minieh*

*Temple of "Wady Saboo"*

### Thursday, Feb. 26

It is very hot. We are floating quickly down the river. It is very pretty. We see at least 60 black and white cranes on one sand-bank. Such a picture. We stop at Wady Saboó-ah to look at the temple, an interesting little temple of the time of Rameses the Great (BC 1400), partly built of sandstone and partly cut into the solid rock behind. There are two statues and eight sphinxes leading up to the pylon, but some of these are buried in the sand, which also fills up the chambers of the temple in the rock. The Arabs call it the Valley of Lions from these sphinxes. We made a little progress after dark.

### Friday, Feb. 27

After an hour or two's rowing, the wind stopt us at

a very dull spot, where we could only improve the shining hours in buying a sheep and a little cow.

*Saturday, Feb. 28*
We see the pretty little temple of Dakkeh. Get a sketch. This was built by Erganum, that wise and plucky Ethiopian king who broke through the very unpleasant rule established by the priests that the king should put an end to his life when the gods desired it and sent a message by them to that effect. He honoured the gods but he paid off the priests and made an end of his own particular lot, slaying them and ruling by his own laws instead. We helped the Neptune off a sandbank and all got stopt by the wind soon after. Mr and Mrs Blood and family. And then they broke our window when we started again.

*Sunday, March 1*
We pass Kalabsha and several notable temples, not being in the humour to see them. We pass the Philae soon after and get to the notable island of Philae at night.

*Monday, March 2*
A long, beautiful day in the temples of Philae. We

have visitors from the Red Boat and Alfred goes shooting with Mr B. junior. On this occasion A. shoots a native instead of his quail—he quails! but the native recovers and the village is satisfied with three shillings backsheesh, which seems cheap for a man.

*Tuesday, March 3*
Another day at Philae. The other d.s disappear from the scene and we follow to Mahatta, a mile down the stream, where there is a small harbour for traders and where the Cataract begins. This day the temples were a prey to Cook's excursionists. Their luncheon party in the adytum was considerably noisy and we saw their facetious gentleman dancing in a red pocket handkerchief on the top of the pylon.

*Wednesday, March 4*
We are all wild with the Reis of the Cataract, who refuses to take us down, Wednesday being an unlucky day. 'Was not a dahabeeiah broken to pieces six years ago on a Wednesday and has he ever taken one since on that unlucky day? No. Nothing would induce him.' So we give it up and row up to see our good friends on the Philae,

which is at anchor at Dabod, where Mr MacCallum is painting beautiful sand drifts. Some of them return with us.

*Thursday, March 5*
Up at six, on deck, boarded by the Reis and his men, the shellaleel. As our old Reis remarked, 'Twenty to row, thirty to scream and ten to direct.' They row us gently down to the head of the cataract, which is no sham this time, and a different passage to the one we came up. We see before us a narrow passage between high granite rocks where the water is regularly roaring for about three hundred yards and with a sudden rush and a bound we are in for it. The great boat gathers fresh impetus every moment, the very Arabs forget to scream for some moments, and just at the last, when we seem to be tearing straight down upon the wall of rocks before us, the steersmen (four of them) give us a good twist and we turn sharp to the left and escape with our lives. The Arabs then gave themselves up to extravagant demonstrations of joy, seized the turbans of some of our men, and salaamed and shook hands with us. They began these manifestations rather too soon and by getting in front of the pilots, who could not see, we

narrowly escaped a great rock in the middle of the rapid towards the end, which as it was we bumped and scraped against considerably and might have got a very similar hole in our side to that the poor crocodile had. After this grand go, we sailed in smooth water for some minutes and then had another rush down another rapid, not so long nor so sheer as the first but sufficiently dangerous, as was proved by the dahabeeiah Dongola which followed us and got a great hole through her on the rocks of this second rapid, causing a stoppage of two days on the spot for repairs before she could be brought to Assouan. We, more fortunate, were now well over our troubles and we glided pleasantly down to Assouan in an hour and a half. The scenery is of course very striking and grand and the morning sunlight made it beautiful. We had

Assooan

all enjoyed our shoot tremendously and after paying our backsheesh like a man were quite ready for breakfast, bazaaring and calling on the Governor, who was holding court as usual under the big sycamore tree at the gate of the town, that fine Ethiopian, Marmoor, who cannot change his skin though he has, alas, changed the cut of his clothes to a short white coat, white trousers and white French boots with black tips. Returning, we meet by accident old Etman, the crocodile hunter from Wady Halfeh. He has just arrived. He declares he

we interview the governor
Joseph harrangues!

was told as he passed Ibreem of the crocodile an Englishman had shot and which had come up on the ninth day, day after our last enquiries! This boils us all up again! We get the Governor Marmoor to telegraph about it to another Gov., who will have to send a man on a camel twenty-four hours' ride for intelligence and so it is *very* uncertain when we shall get even an answer to our telegram. We will not dare to hope for more!!!

*Friday, March 6*
A Mr Chester, sharp in antiquities, calls. We have a grub at Elephantine, that pretty island opposite, where stood two fine old temples not more than 60 years ago, which a governor of that day pulled down to build himself an house at Assouan. It is a heap of heaps of earth and fragments of pottery of all dates, Egyptian, Greek, Saracenic. Some pieces with Greek writing in a flowing hand are found and considered curious. Mr Chester had forestalled us. Abdallah got us a nice old alabaster mortar from here. Then we rowed about amongst the rocks in pursuit of the cranes who judiciously outmanoeuvred us in every corner. An immense flock of black and white cranes were seen a long way off.

Island of
Elephantine

*Saturday, March 7*
No telegram. Tel Hami calls. We hand over the
affair to him and make a start at one o'clock, only
to stick at the sandbank near the telegraph office at
three by reason of contrary winds. Let no one who
has not patience come to the Nile, and let everybody who has!

*Sunday, March 8*
Go about 10 miles. Wind south and strong.

*Monday, March 9*
Stuck fast all day.

*Tuesday, March 10*

Get on pretty well. Have a couple of hours at Kom Ombos, that beautiful temple on the cliff which is half buried in the sand and threatened with final destruction by being undermined by the river. It is similar in style to Philae, built by a Ptolemy some-body and finished by a somebody Caesar. It is, we almost think, the most picturesque ruin we've seen. A good deal of that beautiful fading green and blue colour is left about it, shades of tour-quoise. Here I found a nice little head of Cleopatra, or a goddess, on a small convenient stone that had rolled half way down to the Nile. I rescued it from further destruction! On at night.

Kom Ombo

*Wednesday, March 11*

Silsilis. The great sandstone quarries by the river on both sides, where all the stone for the temples and buildings of Egypt was quarried; some small chapels and grottoes with columns, inscriptions and sculptures are cut in the solid rock. Very interesting, some from their great antiquity, specially those of King Horus as a young prince fed by Isis and as a King carried in triumph with fan bearers. Fans like those of the Pope's. Fine figures, astonishing from their remote age. There are also poems to the Nile God in hieroglyphics. The very stones from the quarries have been so carefully cut away in squares that it is surprising to see the work. Good rowing in the afternoon. We pass the ruined Fortress of Booyab (Saracen) and get stuck on a sandbank, where it takes all hands till the middle of the night to get us off.

*Thursday, March 12*

Edfou. Here is a large and magnificent temple, the best preserved in Egypt, having its great court and pylons and all its columns and chambers and passages and roof complete. It has not long been dug out by Mariette Bey from under an Arab village which is cleared away for some distance round it.

The pylons are immense but we do not like pylons. The view from the top is very pretty of the country and river. We find today that the mad cook has beaten his kitchen maid again. This is about the 10th time, so we tell him if he does it again he must leave at Luxor. Upon this he attempts to precipitate himself into the Nile and is held by the sailors and failing that he departs to the village to see the Governor, who refers him to him at Luxor. And so we go on, not caring, as the K.M., we believe, can cook quite as well.

*Friday, March 13*
At El Kab (Eleithrias). Tombs in the rocks very good, of the XVIII[th] dynasty. Many curious subjects sculptured in them. First, a reception: lady and gentleman sitting on the same chair, to which a pet monkey is tied, receive their guests, entertain them with music, are capital figures. Opposite are all sorts of agricultural subjects — sowing, reaping and thrashing. Here (as at Thebes) is the song in hieroglyphics over the picture. Then there are fishing scenes, boats on the Nile, one with a carriage on deck, wine-making, weaving; almost everything that the old Egyptians could do is represented. The sculptured room leads generally into

a smaller one, in which was the well, 12 to 20 feet deep, at the bottom of which the mummy lay. All is cut in the solid rock and the well most carefully concealed, but everywhere the mummy has been unearthed and all is empty. Persians, Romans, Greeks, all the successive conquerors of Egypt are to blame for this, and if they had not done it the British Museum would, but not for greed! At night we are four miles from Esneh.

### Saturday, March 14

High wind against us. Send men to Esneh to bake. 300 pelicans on a bank close to the boat early in the morning. Sailors too distracted to remember the word 'pelican'. Could only shout to Alfred, 'You get plenty.' He was too late with his rifle.

### Sunday, March 15

We walk to Esneh. Market. Evening, wind goes

" you got plenty "—

down but men keep us waiting four hours and then wind gets up again. Stormy night.

*Monday, March 16*
A whirlwind. We are anchored 8 miles below Esneh, then start at night.

*Tuesday, March 17*
A good day's work. Luxor and Thebes at last.

*Wednesday, March 18*
A day on donkeys amongst the ruins of Thebes. We cross in the felucca and are at once enveloped in a whirlwind of donkey-boys and donkies. Our sailors rescue the fragments and start us off with one

Said. We visit first the temples of Medinet Haboo. These are very grand, the sculptures on the walls very fine and historical. Some parts were built by that Pharoah who defeated Senacharib, some by Amun-noo-ket, that great daughter of Thotmes who raised the obelisk at Karnac and built also the temple of Dayr el Bahree (the sweetest thing in white limestone and sculpture) to the memory of her father. Other parts by Rameses III and, of course, the Ptolemies had a hand in them afterwards, completing and adding on to the original structures. Next we rode to the Ramesium (Memnonium). This great temple with magnificent columns like the last is open to the sky, roofless. It is the great record of the warlike doings of Rameses II. Several of his battles are well sculptured on the walls and the names as well as the costumes of the enemy are of historical interest. I copy from Murray: 'These sculptures are strong corroborative proof of the correctness of the evidence contained in the Bible of the foreign wars and conquests of Egypt.' And both write their testimony in showing that the earlier and more potent Kings of Egypt had subdued all the countries up to and about the River Euphrates. The foreign garb and features and lighter complexion of the captives brought in

" Backsheesh ya Howagha "

triumphal procession go chiefly to prove this.

*Thursday, March 19*
Luxor. A very windy day. We do nothing but visit old Mustapha Agha, British Consul, and look at his scarabs and then to the Prussian Consul's and he shows us some very nice things.

*Friday, March 20*
We go to the other side again: Dayr el Bahr and Dayr el Medina, two pretty little temples beautifully situated part way up the slope of the rock, above which tower the grand old crags of the mountain and from which we have a splendid view across the plain back to the river, with Luxor and Karnac beyond.

*Saturday, March 21*

Again across and to the gorge behind the mountains where are the Tombs of the Kings. A long
hot ride of five or six miles, but the rocks were
grand and we were well repaid by what we saw.
First, the Tomb of Sethos, that Pharoah at whose
court Joseph was prime minister. It is the larg-
est and best preserved of all, running 470 yards
into the mountain, with many chambers cut in
the rock and sculptured elaborately and painted
with many scenes in which the King is present in
the midst of the gods, especially the gods of the
dead, Osiris the great judge and others. One of the
most interesting of these chambers is one where
the paintings were left unfinished. Here we see
that the figures were first roughly sketched in red
and then altered and corrected, probably by the
master's hand, before being left for the sculptor to
chisel out. The drawing is so free and masterly and
it has been noticed here and in other antique drawing that the aim seemed to be to make the long-
est possible single stroke at once, not touching it
again. Possibly the death of the King or some other
cause interfered with the completion of the work.
The grand hall contained a beautiful sarcophagus
of alabaster now in the Soane Museum and it was

a happy accident to Belzoni that, hearing a hollow sound, he was induced to have some part of the wall of the passage knocked through and so discovered it in all its splendour, fresh colours on the walls and roofs and the grand sarcophagus in the middle. Fifty years' exposure have much injured it. The savans have knocked off the cartouches and other wise men have washed off the paint with their nasty squeezes of damp paper, and the water has rushed in at times but still there is very much that is amazingly fresh and curious to behold.

The next tomb they call Bruce's because discovered by that gentleman, as the first is called Belzoni's. It is that of Rameses III and resembles the other in many ways. The scenes on the walls however are more varied. There are agricultural pictures and a great many representations of the Nile and also of furniture and weapons and utensils, very quaint and curious. Some women playing harps are peculiarly strange and altogether it is a most interesting place. We went into several other tombs. I think there are hundreds open but there came a time when we all said 'enough' and that was luncheon time and so in the entrance of some great man's last house we had our chickens and bread, and the donkeys and the little girls who

at the Tombs of the Kings.

had run beside us all the way with water jars on
their heads and the guides and all of us enjoyed
the shade and the quiet and the scraps. We had just
before met a party of American missionaries — two
very stout, florid men and another stout, rather
nice sort of woman, who was much out of breath
coming up from the tombs. We were interested in
their account of themselves selling good books in
Arabic in their snug little dahabeeiah and preach-
ing to a few Copts and combining the pleasures of
a little trip on the Nile with a little good work, or at

least good intentions to their darker brethren, but we did not like them so much for painting 'Jesus Christ 1874' in large letters amongst other promiscuous autographs over the tomb where they had lunched and left their empty bottles and sandwich papers behind them. Why should they do it?

I have omitted to notice the Colossi, those two huge figures of Amunoph III which sit near together in the middle of the plain below the Memnonium. We often passed and were much impressed by their quiet dignity and size. Seventy feet high is as much as any man might reasonably wish to see himself sitting in a sandstone arm-chair, his wife and mother standing by no higher than the elbows. I suppose the Kings of that day liked it, as they seem no sooner to have had one big stone cut for a portrait than they ordered another or two to match. The date of this King's reign is somewhere between 1700 and 1400 BC according to Mariette, and we have a large scarab (something broken by the rim) we luckily purchased at Keneh — found, they said, at Kopt — on which are the figures and cartouches of this same Amunoph and his Queen, and which we believe to be of the same date and undoubtedly genuine. One of these Colossi is known as the Vocal Memnon. It used to emit a strange sound at sunrise when visited by some happy votary who was favoured by the gods, and there are inscriptions upon it recording some of these events. In the time of the Romans it was often visited by grand personages. The Emperor Hadrian was honoured so far as to have the sound repeated three times. Evidently the statue thought, 'such visitors don't come every day' and this confirms the idea that it was altogether a priestly manoeuvre, for the figure had been broken in pieces by falling during an earthquake and in mending it they had probably made a small chamber inside large enough for a man to stand in and work the oracle, and indeed it may be seen at this day. The sound it is said was like the breaking of a harp's string. Mr MacCallum was painting another picture of them but not to equal the one he exhibited last year, we thought.

*Sunday, March 22*
A day of rest at Luxor. The Philae arrived in the afternoon.

*Monday, March 23*
We spent some time with our friends on the Philae, made the acquaintance of the Rosses and pottered about.

*Tuesday, March 24*

We called upon Joseph's marah (wife) and were entertained by him with a bottle of Bass's best in a sort of pig stye yard in front of his house. We sat on a kind of ricketty cane bedstead over which a mat was thrown. By sitting well in the middle and keeping our legs up, we managed not [to] break it. The wife peeped out of the door shyly enough. She had handsome gold ornaments and was a nice clean looking woman, a very good specimen of the kind, and her little dark room had more mats and water jars in it than many others and she became quite at home in the end. Joseph did the honours very well. Afterwards we had a similar entertainment at Abdel Medgid's. This was at night. He gave us coffee and said if Alfred and Joseph would retire, his wife would like to come and speak to us. So those dangerous individuals removed themselves and the little woman came out of her den, a pretty, almost fair complexioned woman in an olive coloured silk gown, with many handsome gold necklaces and earrings and many silver rings on her fingers. She seemed very shy also, but curious about our things.

*Monday*\*
Very windy. Stopt at home.

*Tuesday*\*
Market day at Luxor and we went through the temples and over the house where Lady Duff Gordon used to live. It has a beautiful view of the mountains and plain of Thebes.

*Wednesday, March 25*
Over to the other side and rode to the Memnonium near which Mariette Bey's men are excavating. They had just bought up a fine mummy from out of a hole twenty feet deep. We were only allowed to look at the outer case. Afterwards they found a number of broken mummy cases and another whole one and some good scarabs. We lunched with Miss E. and R. in the Memnonium. Alfred found a wooden face and a silver gersch (small coin) in the toes of the prostrate Rameses, the granite figure which lies at full length (70 feet) on the sand hard by. Very hot, quiet afternoon on the Bagstones afterwards.

---

\* No dates given— extra entries for March 23 and 24?

### Thursday, March 26
Karnac by moonlight, rowing there and back in the felucca — charming. The ruins are indescribably beautiful by moonlight and before the afterglow is quite over. Disturbed night.

### Friday, March 27
Karnac again by day. Another night. We are ready to start and of course, after nine calm days or with wind which would have helped us down the river, there has sprung up a gale from the north.

### Saturday, March 28
Very windy. We cannot start. We take leave of everybody and everybody says it's no use, we shall never get off.

### Sunday, March 29
At last we leave Luxor. At breakfast time Foddle and Said go back without leave to Luxor, ten miles, not thinking that the wind will go down and let us move on. We do, however, and get to Keneh the morning after.

### Monday, March 30
At Keneh. We dispute with the Governor over a

*changing money at Keneh.*

ten pound note and we call on our friend Hassaeen Bey, who sends for Governor and money lender and gets it at a more moderate interest for us, ten shillings instead of twenty. We intended to have taken two sailors in place of the deserters but the sheikh offers us two so old, one-eyed and evil looking that we reject them with horror. Ride back to the dahabeeiah (3 miles) and buy a grand scarab of Amunoph III and Queen, cartouches and all on it, for a moderate sum of money, a bottle of castor oil and an old railway reading lamp of Alfred's. The deserters appear on the shore about Denderah. We refuse to take them on board. That night, the last act in the M. is performed. A storm comes on immediately. The duffer drives us wild, everybody rambles about the ship in search of quiet camping ground. A. and M.I.B. occupy corners of the saloon and M.B. seeks refuge in A.'s cabin. In fact, it is a general exchange.

*Tuesday, March 31*
At Dishnah we take on one of the recreants, Foddle. A good day's rowing. Are stopt by wind in the afternoon just short of Kasr es Said.

*Wednesday, April 1*
Farshoot. Great wind. It goes down and after some row we persuade the sailors to row for just ten minutes. We go four miles or so and then get stuck in a windy corner but it has convinced us that if they had a will there is a way even in windy weather of getting down the Nile. At sunset, the other dahabeeiah coming down, our men make another start but oh it is hard work for the patience and these men we have been so kind to and liked so well will not make any exertion to get us along.

*Thursday, April 2*
We anchor at Bellianch for Abydos, a ride of eight miles across the plain to the temples. We have no

bridles on our donkeys (at least the others had none) but it was very pleasant and the temples well repaid us: so fresh in colour and subjects, some of Mariette's newest excavations. The Salle des Ancêtres, however, seems to have been carefully buried up again, by his orders we suppose. At night we got to Girgeh.

*Friday, April 3*
We have to waste four or five precious hours at Girgeh in a calm paying off Mr Said. The wind rises the moment we start. We meet the Dongola sailing back to Girgeh minus six sailors. Mrs Ross and her sister come to see us and tell how their men refused to row at night even in a dead calm and

Mr Ross was so exasperated he fired his revolver in the air, on which the sailors jumped overboard and got on land. When they offered to return he would not have them and so they were returning for a fresh supply. His captain, too, was a wretch who amongst other enormities had married a young lady of eleven years old at Luxor without even inviting Mr Ross to the wedding.

*Saturday, April 4*
We have got to Shoohag. Here we passed Mr Bentley's boat with a string of crocodiles hung on the mast... alas for us! Very windy all day and night.

*Sunday, April 5*
Fahtah. Wind against us by day and the men so *naughty* that if we leave them rowing and go to bed they do so too!

*Monday, April 6*
Ditto ditto. Sand banks but we escape them, very luckily.

*Tuesday, April 7*
At last at Assiout. The valliant Goggles having volunteered (when no one else would) to walk on 12

miles the day before, has got the bread baked and all ready by eight o'clock. We admire him more than ever, the smallest man you could see anywhere, with the best heart and pluck possible. At last we have a calm day and the sailors condescend to row a little and so we get on. Send a letter to Mr Ralph threatening to leave the boat at Minieh.

*Wednesday, April 8*
Get to Rhoda at night, the sailors having changed their minds at last and rowed well.

*Thursday, April 9*
We stop at Beni Hassan, 11 miles from Rhoda, to see the famous tombs from which Sir Gardner Wilkinson has taken many of his illustrations of the manners and customs of the Ancient Egyptians. The colours unfortunately are fast fading away. The idea that one of the subjects was that of Joseph presenting his brethren to Pharaoh has had to be given up, as the tomb is proved to be that of some governor who lived several centuries previous to Joseph. It is intensely hot. We are going along now very well. It is five (six) o'clock and something cooler than it has been. I get up to look at the thermometer which hangs in a shady

The M.Bs in the Ferry boat at Bedreshayn.

corner and I find it is suffering from heat as much
as any of us, though not so much from the flies,
and it stands at 89 d.

At Minieh M.I.B. and myself left the dahabeeiah
and, taking the faithful Joseph as bodyguard,
departed by train to Cairo. We made a pleasant journey of it in six hours, glad to escape the
monotony of the dried up river and the sad brown
looking palms, and leaving Alfred and George in
full possession. We enjoined our sailors to bring
the boat on as quickly as they could but it was a six
days job for them, as it proved, the wind against

them and even when in sight of Cairo at last, the Old Reis, ever anxious to detain us that his pay might be increased, managed to run the Bagstones on a sand bank for an extra day and night.

Meantime we lodged at the Hotel du Nil, in the centre of the town, and found it, when once reached down that rather dubious passage out of the Moosquee, a most pleasant place, an Eastern garden of exotics round which a square of kiosk-like buildings formed the hotel. Many Nile friends who had agreed with us to cut the ancient glories and especial bad cooking of Shepherd's were here: Mr Frank Dillon, artist, the Fonce de Lornes, Mr Brabazon's party and others, and Col. Maxwell and his wife and young Mills, whom we afterwards met at Jerusalem. Mr Dillon showed us his drawings and introduced us to the beautiful old hall he was painting, a Moslem sanctum difficult of approach. The master, like others, is letting his grand old house fall to pieces from neglect and decay while he is jealous of intrusion from a Christian painter who would preserve at least a remembrance of its marble mosaics, stained glass windows and painted roof. We met also Mr E. Frère, a French artist, very clever. We much enjoyed our week, albeit Mr MacCallum was gone to England and the rest of the Philae party had not arrived. We prowled in the bazaars from morn till eve and in the Museum, ticketted off our treasures.

At last the Bagstones arrived and, with Mr Ralph's assistance, got our goods and chattels off the same day and railed away to Alexandria, our beloved mummy and papyrus (for full account of which see Apendix) safely smuggled under the nose of suspicion—which nose afterwards thought it smelt a rat and caused the other boxes to be opened and ransacked—and so we were ready for a start next day, having engaged as dragoman Elias Abas, Syrian from Mt Lebanon, to conduct us through Palestine, by Damascus and over the Lebanon to Beyrout.

Here I must record with sadness the death of our chamelion, who the night before reaching Cairo swallowed a poisoned fly, to the great grief of the trio with whom he had lived on such friendly terms for nearly three months, and I must also mention in a melancholy manner that Joseph 'the faithful', never before suspected guilty of the shadow of turning, save once to the tune of two-pence, here tried to do us in the matter of buying a tarboosh and it being brought to light was fain to confess with tears of his sins and was punished by the loss of some of his backsheesh. Poor Joseph, a faithful old slavy, but greedy, and let us not be hard on his memory considering that, like the rest of the sailors, his pay was only thirty shillings a month for three or four months at the most and then nothing to do or to get until the next season began.

*Friday, April 17*
Adieu to Cairo. After all our wanderings we look back upon it as the most enchanting city in the world, with its narrow streets, its party coloured mosks and minarets far sweeter than those of Constantinople or Damascus, its shady, gleamy bazaars and motly coloured crowds. We never shall see thy like again! Oh Cairo!

We journey together to Alexandria, are very sleepy and very cross with an ugly looking fat Egyptian who gets in unexpectedly. We try to turn him out with the help of dragoman Abas and don't succeed. He turns out indeed to be the Governor of Alexandria and talks English as well as we do. He brought the first hippopotamus to England, he says, and we become very friendly in the long run, and very well we do perhaps!!! At Alexandria, Abbats Hotel is full and we sleep in new rooms in damp beds and M.I.B. suffers for it afterwards — all through Syria.

*Saturday, April 18*
We are very busy taking tickets for ourselves to Jaffa and for Alfred to Venice, he to sail on Monday while we have to depart by the Messagerie Steamer, La Bourdonnais, this very afternoon. We present a long pipe à la Turc to Alfred and take our leave with much regret at breaking up the happy little party wot has woyaged up and down the Nile together.

*Sunday, April 19*
We stop all day at Port Said, we two M.B.s picnicking on the banks of the Suez Canal, picking up coral from the Red Sea and prowling on the shore of Lake Manzalee, where dead flamingoes lie about on the sand. A good passage we have had, and another in prospect, and so good bye to old Egypt!

# Appendix

*How We Got Our Mummy*

It was on board the Simla as we lay in quarrantine at Alexandria that we first heard of this interesting creature. A celebrated artist, whose tent had baked under many an Egyptian sun and whose love of antiquities and popularity among the Arabs had made him acquainted with various treasures hid away in their caves, promised to introduce us to this one, should it happen that fate brought us together on the spot at the same time...

Curiously enough, it did so happen and the M.B.s riding among the ruins of Thebes were hailed by a friendly call of 'Hie there, Bagstones', proceeding from a tent in which sat the artist hard at work and not a hundred and fifty miles off as they had thought. The result was a halt, a chat, the leg of a chicken and a glass of Bourdeaux, and the sun going down and the donkey boys being disposed of in another direction, we stole off together on foot through the fields of ripening barley and little peas and scrambled in the dark up the rocky hill above those noble ruins which stand upon the desert to the house — or rather tomb, for rock-cut tomb it was—where the Arab family in question resided. A series of chambers cut in the solid rock and running deep into the hill, where the old hieroglyphics showed in places through the modern plaster of mud, was the rendezvous.

Here we had Kalam and coffee of a horrid description which we felt bound to take in compliment to our hosts. One of the party, I am sorry to say, poured hers out in a dark corner but the ground dryly refused to swallow such an affront to Arab hospitality and let it trickle in a narrow, tale-telling stream to the very feet of our entertainers, who politely took no notice. We then proceeded underground through several rooms, each hotter and hotter like a Turkish bath, to an upper den, to which we were hoisted perhaps twelve or fifteen feet high by the strong arms of our black friends. The sort of large chimney we went up had no purchase for our poor feet, so we were completely off them and more like clappers in a bell than anything else I can think of. Here we found the Mummy in its very prettily painted case (white ground and coloured figures) and all enclosed in a wooden sarcophagus more than an inch in thickness, which from its size and weight was necessarily out of all question in a smuggling point of view.

The case did not appear to belong to a mummy of great importance, having no gold on the outside; it was about five feet long. We liked its looks, however, and we liked the idea of smuggling on a large scale under the nose of the Pasha's guards who, as excavations were then going on near at hand, were pretty thick on the ground and on the alert.

We returned alone with our friendly Arabs, a four miles ride in the dark to the dahabeeiah, leaving Mr Maguilp R.A. to do the bargaining for us, he having something on hand of his own besides. If successful, he was to bring the Mummy to us in the night and land it through our cabin window. Thus we sat up the first night watching, but in vain, nothing came of it, and M.R.A., departing early next morning with the Duke who was expediting his return, could make no sign.

Afterwards, we were left to our own devices and had many secret interviews with the proprietors. Again we visited their den, this time to see a fine papyrus which finally was included in the bargain—first price asked was a hundred pounds for the two! But now we got entangled with another Arab who wished to act as go between and have a finger in the profits and whom we had reason afterwards to suspect of treachery, of informing against us to a man in authority, but I think we propitiated both by a present of champagne and cognac and by purchasing some doubtful antiques at a good price.

Some days elapsed ere the bargain was finished and a good round number of sovereigns could be got together and paid down, as no Arab recognizes a bank note or a guinea with King George on it as of any note whatever. At last it was all arranged. Alfred and George were to steal off in the felucca after the moon had set and receive the Mummy on the opposite shore, the Arabs bringing it there, carrying it at least four miles and running the gauntlet of all M. Mariette's guards, and then, as it was of the utmost consequence that our sailors should know nothing about it, we were to receive it in at the window of our cabin. Thus we waited and watched the second night, all lights out, A. and G. asleep in their clothes but ready for action.

At one o'clock we saw a boat with six men row across quickly to the other side, land the men and quietly return. We did not like the looks of it but at three the moon went down and our promise must be kept, so directly afterwards A. and G. got out of our window and crept along the edge of the dahabeeiah to the felucca, which fastened to the rudder. This was not loosened without sundry bumps, which gave a shock to our nervous systems. They started but were scarcely off when, dark as it was, they must have been seen for a gun was fired from our side the river not far below us, evidently a signal. We struck three convulsive matches, the sign of danger agreed upon, and they came back. A. and G. were for trying again but when we had taken into consideration that the freedom, the property, almost the lives of the poor fellows over the way depended on our prudence, they agreed it was better to give it up for that night. Mariette Bey is said to be very stern and cruel with these contrabandists if he catches them, though it is also whispered that in the capacity of Conservator of the Antiquities of Egypt, he manages to do a little that way on his own account, and that not a few little things find themselves in the Paris Museum instead of in that of Boulac.

Half an hour elapsed and a gun was fired from the opposite side; a boat was again heard crossing the stream. At day break another boat passed with two men who rowed close round our dahabeeiah. It was an awful thought that perhaps our Arab friends had been caught, Mummy and all, and might be in the hands of the police but there was nothing further that we could do till next day, when we had to look as innocent as we could — very glad we were to find the men and Mummy had escaped. They had brought it over to our side, a long way down the river, and had carried it to the house of a friend not far off, the same house from which we had smuggled the papyrus away in the sleeve of a thick Inverness coat the night previous — a very hot night too and if Arabs had brains, which they haven't, it might have struck some one as an odd thing to wear on such occasion. Now we learnt that the second gun had been fired by the expectant Arabs, who had imagined the first shot to be a signal of our departure. How they had escaped, and how far we were involved and watched was therefore still a horrible mystery. It hung over us like the sword by the single hair.

However, we determined to have another try and it was agreed that George and one of the Arabs were to carry the Mummy down to our boat after dark and put it in at the window, this time from the land side. Again we watched. We had a midnight supper in which ham fortunately predominated, for we fell asleep soon after and had it not been for the ham and consequent nightmares we should never have woke up till morning. Again, the impatience of the Arabs nearly spoilt all. They got tired of waiting till the moon set and one came cautiously on board and called up George. They went away together. We saw it all in an agony of mind but it was too late to interfere. Presently we saw them coming down the bank carrying the horrid thing wrapt in a black cloth all in the bright moonshine. Very luckily none of the sailors were roused but we mentally resolved to have no more secret well laid plots with Arabs! The Mummy was deposited in the passage, where one of us stumbled over it in the dark, the bearer was thrust out of the window and all was over!

And now we had our Mummy safe in our cabin. He looked when we removed the cloth quite pretty in all his paint and hieroglyphics. We declared him to be altogether a festive object and not at all a funereal old frump and, being quite done up with excitement and fatigue, we soon fell asleep, with our new friend standing up in the middle of our small apartment. Next day we hid him in the linen closet, carefully securing both window and door, and very anxious [we] were to set sail as soon as possible but the wind turned dead against us and it was not until the day but one after that we got away from the dread spot.

The next thing to be done was the all important operation of sawing up the case, which was accomplished successfully by M.I.B. who had bought a little saw for the purpose at the last town. When the line round the case had been sawn through, the top was lifted up and the thrilling moment arrived — when our hopes were scattered by finding the mummy of a little boy, about 12 years old, no ornaments, papyrus, scarabs, not even a little god or two had been placed on his little person. We supposed they thought him too innocent to need such help on his journey to heaven, from where, I trust, if he looked down upon our proceedings, he felt no bitterness of wrath. The bandages of cloth we carefully wrapt round him again; they must have been fifty or sixty yards in length. There was some writing on the little shirt (probably his name) which was fringed round. His skin was hard and dry and shiny like good old oak and the features of his face were really pleasant and happy in expression and there was hair on his woodeny little head. The little Mummy was buried by night with great secrecy and left in his native land.

Once more safely boxed up, we devoutly hoped it (*the case* only) might escape the prying fingers of the dreaded police who were waiting for us at

Cairo, at Alexandria, everywhere, all suspicious of the Hawagha on the Nile. We were right glad when we had got finished as, whether from the bitumen and spices with which the case was cemented inside or what, there had been a suspicious odour in the passage near the closet where the Mummy was concealed and we feared lest the cook in particular, who had been in the service of Mariette Bey himself and doubtless was acquainted with the peculiar mummy 'bouquet', might sniff him out and bring us all to grief.

### The Sequel

On the arrival of the dahabeeiah at Cairo, we hurried on board and with Mr Ralph's assistance got all our valuables, which were ready boxed, on shore and the guards unsuspectingly let them pass on their way to the Railway Station, but the next lot, which we had to pack and bring later, attracted their notice and we had to submit to all being turned out on the high road, lamps and kettles and blankets and all sorts of things. We grumbled openly but secretly rejoiced to think that our Mummy and other little friends were safely waiting for us at the station. At Alexandria we were equally fortunate and got everything bribed on board the steamer without difficulty, but that there is a good deal of chance about it, that we were lucky whilst others are not, has been since shown in the case of our friends on the Philae, who had all their antiquities seized at Alexandria and are doubtful if they will ever be able to recover them, even with Mr Ralph's assistance. So ends my tale.

*Opposite:* First page of a letter pasted into the diary, with this note from Marianne:

*Letter from Dr. Birch (British Museum) informing us that our Mummy was 'a young girl, a singer in the inner sanctuary of a temple', and not a boy as we supposed.*

3d June 1875

Dear Miss Brocklehurst

Your friend Mrs
Fielden I hope accompanied
you on the occasion but I have
been so occupied as to have had
no time to answer you till
Today. The inscription contain
the name of the lady for
whom the coffin was made
"Sheb-mut singer of the interior
room" or "hall" of the palace or

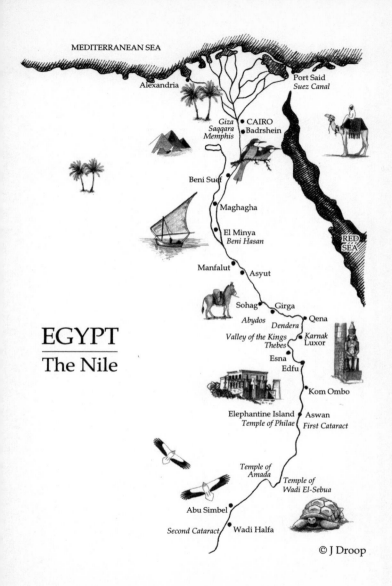

MEDITERRANEAN SEA

Alexandria

Port Said
*Suez Canal*

*Giza*
*Saqqara*
*Memphis*
CAIRO
Badrshein

Beni Suef

Maghagha

El Minya
*Beni Hasan*

RED
SEA

Manfalut
Asyut

Sohag
Girga

*Abydos*
*Dendera*
Qena

*Valley of the Kings*
*Thebes*
*Karnak*
Luxor

Esna
Edfu

Kom Ombo

Elephantine Island
*Temple of Philae*
Aswan
*First Cataract*

# EGYPT
## The Nile

*Temple of*
*Amada*
*Temple of*
*Wadi El-Sebua*

Abu Simbel

*Second Cataract*
Wadi Halfa

© J Droop